50 Japan Winter Cookies Recipes for Home

By: Kelly Johnson

Table of Contents

- Matcha Shortbread Cookies
- Black Sesame Cookies
- Sweet Potato Cookies
- Yuzu Citrus Cookies
- Miso Caramel Cookies
- Red Bean Paste Cookies
- Gingerbread Cookies with Japanese Spices
- Sakura Blossom Cookies
- Taro Cookies
- Kabocha Squash Cookies
- Sesame Almond Cookies
- Uji Matcha Biscotti
- Kinako (Roasted Soy Flour) Cookies
- Japanese Cheesecake Cookies
- Mochi Cookies
- Japanese Sweet Potato and Nut Cookies
- Yatsuhashi Cookies
- Soy Sauce Caramel Cookies
- Plum Wine Cookies
- Choco-Banana Mochi Cookies
- Azuki Bean and Walnut Cookies
- Green Tea and White Chocolate Cookies
- Shiso Leaf Cookies
- Chestnut and Maple Cookies
- Wasabi and Sesame Cookies
- Miso and Brown Sugar Cookies
- Sake-Infused Cookies
- Japanese Spiced Butter Cookies
- Sweet Soy Glazed Cookies
- Japanese Plum Cookies
- Black Sugar Cookies
- Yuzu and Ginger Cookies

- Tamarind and Coconut Cookies
- Japanese Pumpkin Pie Cookies
- Matcha and Red Bean Cookies
- Kinako and Black Sesame Cookies
- Sesame and Honey Cookies
- Sweet Potato and Cinnamon Cookies
- Cherry Blossom Macarons
- Matcha Swirl Cookies
- Mochi Rice Flour Cookies
- Japanese Green Tea Shortbread
- Red Bean Mochi Cookies
- Shiso and Lime Cookies
- Yuzu and White Chocolate Cookies
- Japanese Green Tea Macarons
- Chestnut and Yuzu Cookies
- Miso and Caramel Crunch Cookies
- Sakura and White Chocolate Cookies
- Kumquat and Almond Cookies

Matcha Shortbread Cookies

Ingredients:

- **For the Cookies**:
    - 1 cup (2 sticks) unsalted butter, softened
    - 1/2 cup granulated sugar
    - 1/4 cup powdered sugar
    - 2 cups all-purpose flour
    - 2 tablespoons matcha green tea powder
    - 1/4 teaspoon salt
    - 1 teaspoon vanilla extract (optional)
- **For Garnish** (optional):
    - Extra granulated sugar for sprinkling
    - Matcha powder for dusting

Instructions:

1. **Prepare the Dough**:
    - **Cream Butter and Sugars**: In a large mixing bowl, use an electric mixer to cream together the softened butter, granulated sugar, and powdered sugar until light and fluffy.
    - **Add Dry Ingredients**: In a separate bowl, whisk together the flour, matcha green tea powder, and salt.
    - **Combine Ingredients**: Gradually add the dry ingredients to the butter mixture, mixing on low speed until just combined. If using, add vanilla extract at this stage.
    - **Form the Dough**: Gather the dough into a ball and flatten it into a disc. Wrap it in plastic wrap and refrigerate for at least 30 minutes to firm up.
2. **Preheat Oven**:
    - **Preheat**: Preheat your oven to 350°F (175°C).
    - **Prepare Baking Sheets**: Line baking sheets with parchment paper.
3. **Roll Out and Cut Cookies**:
    - **Roll Dough**: On a lightly floured surface, roll out the chilled dough to about 1/4-inch thickness.
    - **Cut Cookies**: Use cookie cutters to cut out shapes from the dough. Alternatively, you can cut the dough into squares or rectangles using a knife.
4. **Bake**:
    - **Transfer Cookies**: Place the cut-out cookies onto the prepared baking sheets, spacing them about 1 inch apart.
    - **Bake**: Bake in the preheated oven for 10-12 minutes, or until the edges are just starting to turn golden brown. The centers should remain pale.
5. **Cool and Garnish**:

- **Cool**: Allow the cookies to cool on the baking sheets for a few minutes before transferring them to wire racks to cool completely.
- **Garnish**: If desired, sprinkle the cooled cookies with extra granulated sugar or dust with a little more matcha powder for added flavor and presentation.

6. **Serve and Enjoy**:
   - Enjoy the cookies with a cup of tea or as a sweet treat anytime.

Tips:

- **Matcha Quality**: Use high-quality matcha powder for the best flavor and vibrant color.
- **Butter**: Make sure the butter is softened to room temperature for easy mixing and a smooth dough.
- **Chilling the Dough**: Chilling the dough helps prevent spreading and makes it easier to cut out shapes.

Matcha Shortbread Cookies are a perfect blend of buttery goodness and the distinct taste of matcha, offering a deliciously unique cookie experience. Enjoy baking and savoring these treats!

Black Sesame Cookies

Ingredients:

- 1 cup (120g) black sesame seeds
- 1 cup (200g) granulated sugar
- 1/2 cup (1 stick, 115g) unsalted butter, softened
- 1 large egg
- 1 1/2 cups (190g) all-purpose flour
- 1/2 teaspoon baking powder
- 1/4 teaspoon salt
- 1/4 cup (60ml) milk
- Optional: 1/2 teaspoon vanilla extract

Instructions:

1. **Preheat Oven:**
   - Preheat your oven to 350°F (175°C) and line a baking sheet with parchment paper.
2. **Prepare Sesame Seeds:**
   - In a dry skillet over medium heat, lightly toast the black sesame seeds until fragrant, about 2-3 minutes. Let them cool, then grind them into a fine powder using a food processor or spice grinder. You can also use pre-ground black sesame powder if available.
3. **Cream Butter and Sugar:**
   - In a large bowl, cream together the softened butter and granulated sugar until light and fluffy.
4. **Add Egg:**
   - Beat in the egg (and vanilla extract if using) until well combined.
5. **Mix Dry Ingredients:**
   - In a separate bowl, whisk together the flour, baking powder, and salt.
6. **Combine Ingredients:**
   - Gradually add the dry ingredients to the butter mixture, mixing until just combined. Stir in the ground black sesame seeds and milk until the dough comes together. It should be slightly soft but not sticky.
7. **Shape Cookies:**
   - Scoop tablespoon-sized portions of dough and roll them into balls. Place them on the prepared baking sheet, spacing them about 2 inches apart. Flatten each ball slightly with the back of a spoon or your fingers.
8. **Bake:**
   - Bake in the preheated oven for 10-12 minutes, or until the edges are golden brown. The centers may still be soft, but they will firm up as they cool.
9. **Cool:**

- Allow the cookies to cool on the baking sheet for a few minutes before transferring them to a wire rack to cool completely.

Tips:

- **Storage:** Store the cookies in an airtight container at room temperature for up to a week.
- **Variation:** For an extra touch, you can sprinkle some extra black sesame seeds on top of the cookies before baking.

Enjoy your homemade black sesame cookies with a cup of tea or coffee!

Sweet Potato Cookies

Ingredients:

- 1 cup (200g) mashed sweet potato (about 1 medium sweet potato)
- 1 cup (200g) granulated sugar
- 1/2 cup (1 stick, 115g) unsalted butter, softened
- 1 large egg
- 1 1/2 cups (190g) all-purpose flour
- 1 teaspoon baking powder
- 1/2 teaspoon baking soda
- 1/2 teaspoon ground cinnamon
- 1/4 teaspoon ground nutmeg
- 1/4 teaspoon salt
- 1/2 cup (60g) chopped nuts or chocolate chips (optional)
- Optional: 1/2 teaspoon vanilla extract

Instructions:

1. **Prepare Sweet Potato:**
   - Peel and cut the sweet potato into chunks. Boil or steam the chunks until tender, about 15 minutes. Drain and mash until smooth. Let the mashed sweet potato cool before using.
2. **Preheat Oven:**
   - Preheat your oven to 350°F (175°C) and line a baking sheet with parchment paper.
3. **Cream Butter and Sugar:**
   - In a large bowl, cream together the softened butter and granulated sugar until light and fluffy.
4. **Add Egg and Sweet Potato:**
   - Beat in the egg and vanilla extract (if using) until well combined. Mix in the mashed sweet potato until smooth.
5. **Mix Dry Ingredients:**
   - In a separate bowl, whisk together the flour, baking powder, baking soda, cinnamon, nutmeg, and salt.
6. **Combine Ingredients:**
   - Gradually add the dry ingredients to the wet mixture, mixing until just combined. Fold in the chopped nuts or chocolate chips if desired.
7. **Shape Cookies:**
   - Scoop tablespoon-sized portions of dough and place them on the prepared baking sheet, spacing them about 2 inches apart. Flatten each ball slightly with the back of a spoon or your fingers.

8. **Bake:**
   - Bake in the preheated oven for 10-12 minutes, or until the edges are golden brown. The centers may still be soft, but they will firm up as they cool.
9. **Cool:**
   - Allow the cookies to cool on the baking sheet for a few minutes before transferring them to a wire rack to cool completely.

Tips:

- **Storage:** Store the cookies in an airtight container at room temperature for up to a week, or freeze for longer storage.
- **Sweet Potato Prep:** You can use canned sweet potato puree for convenience if you prefer.
- **Variations:** Feel free to add spices like ginger or cloves for additional flavor, or mix in raisins or coconut flakes for a twist.

Enjoy these soft, flavorful cookies with a glass of milk or a hot cup of tea!

Yuzu Citrus Cookies

Ingredients:

- 1 cup (2 sticks, 230g) unsalted butter, softened
- 3/4 cup (150g) granulated sugar
- 1/2 cup (100g) brown sugar, packed
- 1 large egg
- 1 tablespoon yuzu juice (fresh or bottled)
- 1 teaspoon yuzu zest (fresh or bottled)
- 2 1/4 cups (285g) all-purpose flour
- 1/2 teaspoon baking soda
- 1/2 teaspoon baking powder
- 1/4 teaspoon salt
- Optional: 1/2 teaspoon vanilla extract

For Glaze (optional):

- 1 cup (120g) powdered sugar
- 2 tablespoons yuzu juice
- 1 teaspoon yuzu zest

Instructions:

1. **Preheat Oven:**
   - Preheat your oven to 350°F (175°C) and line a baking sheet with parchment paper.
2. **Cream Butter and Sugars:**
   - In a large bowl, cream together the softened butter, granulated sugar, and brown sugar until light and fluffy.
3. **Add Egg and Yuzu:**
   - Beat in the egg until well combined. Then mix in the yuzu juice and zest. If using vanilla extract, add it here as well.
4. **Mix Dry Ingredients:**
   - In a separate bowl, whisk together the flour, baking soda, baking powder, and salt.
5. **Combine Ingredients:**
   - Gradually add the dry ingredients to the wet mixture, mixing until just combined. Do not overmix.
6. **Shape Cookies:**
   - Scoop tablespoon-sized portions of dough and place them on the prepared baking sheet, spacing them about 2 inches apart. Flatten each ball slightly with the back of a spoon or your fingers.

7. **Bake:**
   - Bake in the preheated oven for 10-12 minutes, or until the edges are lightly golden. The centers may still be soft.
8. **Cool:**
   - Allow the cookies to cool on the baking sheet for a few minutes before transferring them to a wire rack to cool completely.
9. **Prepare Glaze (Optional):**
   - In a small bowl, mix the powdered sugar with the yuzu juice and zest until smooth. Drizzle or spread the glaze over the cooled cookies. Let the glaze set before serving.

Tips:

- **Yuzu Juice:** If fresh yuzu is unavailable, bottled yuzu juice can be found at Asian grocery stores or online. You can also substitute with lemon or lime juice in a pinch, though the flavor will be different.
- **Storage:** Store the cookies in an airtight container at room temperature for up to a week. If glazed, store in a single layer to prevent the glaze from sticking.

These yuzu citrus cookies offer a delightful balance of sweetness and tang, perfect for adding a touch of citrusy brightness to your day!

Miso Caramel Cookies

Ingredients:

- 1 cup (2 sticks, 230g) unsalted butter, softened
- 1 cup (200g) granulated sugar
- 1/2 cup (100g) brown sugar, packed
- 1 large egg
- 2 tablespoons white miso paste
- 1 teaspoon vanilla extract
- 2 1/4 cups (285g) all-purpose flour
- 1/2 teaspoon baking soda
- 1/2 teaspoon baking powder
- 1/4 teaspoon salt
- 1 cup (170g) caramel bits or chopped soft caramel candies

For Drizzle (Optional):

- 1/2 cup (80g) caramel sauce
- 1 tablespoon milk (or as needed to thin)
- 1/4 teaspoon sea salt (optional, for sprinkling)

Instructions:

1. **Preheat Oven:**
   - Preheat your oven to 350°F (175°C) and line a baking sheet with parchment paper.
2. **Cream Butter and Sugars:**
   - In a large bowl, cream together the softened butter, granulated sugar, and brown sugar until light and fluffy.
3. **Add Egg, Miso, and Vanilla:**
   - Beat in the egg until well combined. Mix in the white miso paste and vanilla extract until smooth.
4. **Mix Dry Ingredients:**
   - In a separate bowl, whisk together the flour, baking soda, baking powder, and salt.
5. **Combine Ingredients:**
   - Gradually add the dry ingredients to the wet mixture, mixing until just combined. Fold in the caramel bits or chopped caramel candies.
6. **Shape Cookies:**
   - Scoop tablespoon-sized portions of dough and place them on the prepared baking sheet, spacing them about 2 inches apart. Flatten each ball slightly with the back of a spoon or your fingers.

7. **Bake:**
    - Bake in the preheated oven for 10-12 minutes, or until the edges are golden brown. The centers may still be soft but will firm up as they cool.
8. **Cool:**
    - Allow the cookies to cool on the baking sheet for a few minutes before transferring them to a wire rack to cool completely.
9. **Prepare Drizzle (Optional):**
    - In a small bowl, mix the caramel sauce with milk until smooth and drizzleable. Drizzle over the cooled cookies and sprinkle with sea salt if desired. Allow the drizzle to set before serving.

Tips:

- **Miso Paste:** Use white miso paste for a milder flavor. You can substitute with other types of miso if you prefer, but the flavor will be more pronounced.
- **Caramel Bits:** If you can't find caramel bits, you can chop up caramel candies into small pieces.
- **Storage:** Store the cookies in an airtight container at room temperature for up to a week. The drizzle can become sticky, so layer the cookies with parchment paper if stacking.

These miso caramel cookies offer a delightful blend of salty and sweet, with a hint of umami that makes them truly special!

Red Bean Paste Cookies

Ingredients:

- 1 cup (2 sticks, 230g) unsalted butter, softened
- 1 cup (200g) granulated sugar
- 1 large egg
- 1/2 teaspoon vanilla extract
- 2 1/4 cups (285g) all-purpose flour
- 1/2 teaspoon baking powder
- 1/4 teaspoon salt
- 1/2 cup (100g) red bean paste (anko)
- 1 tablespoon milk (optional, for dough consistency)

For Topping (Optional):

- 1 tablespoon sesame seeds or a small amount of coarse sugar

Instructions:

1. **Preheat Oven:**
   - Preheat your oven to 350°F (175°C) and line a baking sheet with parchment paper.
2. **Cream Butter and Sugar:**
   - In a large bowl, cream together the softened butter and granulated sugar until light and fluffy.
3. **Add Egg and Vanilla:**
   - Beat in the egg and vanilla extract until well combined.
4. **Mix Dry Ingredients:**
   - In a separate bowl, whisk together the flour, baking powder, and salt.
5. **Combine Ingredients:**
   - Gradually add the dry ingredients to the wet mixture, mixing until just combined. If the dough is too dry or crumbly, add a tablespoon of milk to help bring it together.
6. **Incorporate Red Bean Paste:**
   - Divide the dough into small balls (about 1 tablespoon each). Flatten each ball slightly and place a small spoonful of red bean paste in the center. Gently fold the edges of the dough around the red bean paste and roll into a ball, sealing the paste inside.
7. **Shape Cookies:**
   - Place the dough balls on the prepared baking sheet, spacing them about 2 inches apart. Flatten each ball slightly with the back of a spoon or your fingers. If desired, sprinkle the tops with sesame seeds or coarse sugar.
8. **Bake:**

- Bake in the preheated oven for 12-15 minutes, or until the edges are lightly golden. The centers should remain soft.
9. **Cool:**
    - Allow the cookies to cool on the baking sheet for a few minutes before transferring them to a wire rack to cool completely.

Tips:

- **Red Bean Paste:** You can use store-bought red bean paste or make your own. For a smoother paste, you can blend it before using. If using homemade red bean paste, ensure it's well-cooked and smooth.
- **Dough Consistency:** If the dough is too soft or sticky, chill it in the refrigerator for about 30 minutes before shaping.
- **Storage:** Store the cookies in an airtight container at room temperature for up to a week. They can also be frozen for longer storage.

These red bean paste cookies offer a delightful combination of sweet, creamy red bean filling and buttery cookie dough, making them a unique and enjoyable treat!

Gingerbread Cookies with Japanese Spices

Ingredients:

- 3 1/4 cups (410g) all-purpose flour
- 1 teaspoon baking soda
- 1 tablespoon ground ginger
- 1 teaspoon ground cinnamon
- 1/2 teaspoon ground cloves
- 1/2 teaspoon ground nutmeg
- 1/2 teaspoon shichimi togarashi (or 1/4 teaspoon sichuan peppercorns, ground, as an alternative)
- 1/4 teaspoon salt
- 1/2 cup (1 stick, 115g) unsalted butter, softened
- 1/2 cup (100g) granulated sugar
- 1/2 cup (100g) packed brown sugar
- 1 large egg
- 1/2 cup (120ml) molasses
- 1 tablespoon yuzu juice (optional, or substitute with orange juice)

For Glaze (Optional):

- 1 cup (120g) powdered sugar
- 2 tablespoons milk or water
- 1/2 teaspoon yuzu juice (optional, or substitute with lemon juice)

Instructions:

1. **Preheat Oven:**
   - Preheat your oven to 350°F (175°C) and line a baking sheet with parchment paper.
2. **Mix Dry Ingredients:**
   - In a large bowl, whisk together the flour, baking soda, ground ginger, cinnamon, cloves, nutmeg, shichimi togarashi (or sichuan peppercorns), and salt.
3. **Cream Butter and Sugars:**
   - In a separate large bowl, cream together the softened butter, granulated sugar, and brown sugar until light and fluffy.
4. **Add Egg and Molasses:**
   - Beat in the egg until well combined. Then mix in the molasses and yuzu juice (if using) until smooth.
5. **Combine Ingredients:**
   - Gradually add the dry ingredients to the wet mixture, mixing until just combined. The dough will be thick.
6. **Roll and Cut Dough:**

- On a lightly floured surface, roll out the dough to about 1/4 inch thickness. Use cookie cutters to cut out shapes and place them on the prepared baking sheet.
7. **Bake:**
    - Bake in the preheated oven for 8-10 minutes, or until the edges are firm and just starting to brown. The centers may still be soft but will firm up as they cool.
8. **Cool:**
    - Allow the cookies to cool on the baking sheet for a few minutes before transferring them to a wire rack to cool completely.
9. **Prepare Glaze (Optional):**
    - In a small bowl, mix the powdered sugar with the milk (or water) and yuzu juice (or lemon juice) until smooth. Drizzle over the cooled cookies and let it set.

Tips:

- **Shichimi Togarashi:** This Japanese spice blend adds a mild heat and complexity. If you prefer less spice, use a smaller amount or omit it.
- **Sichuan Peppercorns:** These add a unique citrusy, numbing heat. Adjust the amount based on your preference.
- **Yuzu Juice:** Adds a citrusy note. If unavailable, lemon or orange juice can be used as substitutes.
- **Storage:** Store the cookies in an airtight container at room temperature for up to a week. They can also be frozen for longer storage.

These gingerbread cookies with Japanese spices bring a delightful twist to the traditional recipe, combining familiar warmth with exciting new flavors!

Sakura Blossom Cookies

Ingredients:

- 1 cup (2 sticks, 230g) unsalted butter, softened
- 1 cup (200g) granulated sugar
- 1 large egg
- 1 teaspoon vanilla extract
- 2 1/4 cups (285g) all-purpose flour
- 1/2 teaspoon baking powder
- 1/4 teaspoon salt
- **1 tablespoon sakura blossom powder** (or sakura extract, or cherry blossom tea leaves finely ground)*
- **Optional: 1/4 cup (30g) finely chopped dried sakura blossoms** (available from specialty Asian stores or online)

For Glaze (Optional):

- 1 cup (120g) powdered sugar
- 2 tablespoons milk or water
- **1 tablespoon sakura blossom syrup** (or cherry blossom extract, if available)**
- **1/4 teaspoon sakura blossom powder** (for garnish, optional)

Instructions:

1. **Preheat Oven:**
   - Preheat your oven to 350°F (175°C) and line a baking sheet with parchment paper.
2. **Cream Butter and Sugar:**
   - In a large bowl, cream together the softened butter and granulated sugar until light and fluffy.
3. **Add Egg and Vanilla:**
   - Beat in the egg and vanilla extract until well combined.
4. **Mix Dry Ingredients:**
   - In a separate bowl, whisk together the flour, baking powder, salt, and sakura blossom powder.
5. **Combine Ingredients:**
   - Gradually add the dry ingredients to the wet mixture, mixing until just combined. If using, fold in the finely chopped dried sakura blossoms.
6. **Shape Cookies:**
   - Scoop tablespoon-sized portions of dough and roll them into balls. Place them on the prepared baking sheet, spacing them about 2 inches apart. Flatten each ball slightly with the back of a spoon or your fingers.
7. **Bake:**

- Bake in the preheated oven for 10-12 minutes, or until the edges are lightly golden. The centers may still be soft but will firm up as they cool.
8. **Cool:**
   - Allow the cookies to cool on the baking sheet for a few minutes before transferring them to a wire rack to cool completely.
9. **Prepare Glaze (Optional):**
   - In a small bowl, mix the powdered sugar with the milk or water and sakura blossom syrup until smooth. Drizzle over the cooled cookies and sprinkle with sakura blossom powder if desired. Allow the glaze to set before serving.

Tips:

- **Sakura Blossom Powder:** You can find sakura blossom powder in specialty Asian grocery stores or online. If unavailable, you can use cherry blossom extract or a small amount of cherry extract as an alternative.
- **Sakura Blossom Syrup:** This can also be found at specialty stores or online. If using extract or syrup, adjust the amount to taste.
- **Dried Sakura Blossoms:** If using dried blossoms, ensure they are food-grade and finely chopped.

These sakura blossom cookies offer a delicate floral flavor and a touch of elegance, making them perfect for special occasions or simply to enjoy a taste of spring!

Taro Cookies

Ingredients:

- 1 cup (2 sticks, 230g) unsalted butter, softened
- 1 cup (200g) granulated sugar
- 1 large egg
- 1 teaspoon vanilla extract
- 1 cup (200g) taro paste (store-bought or homemade)**
- 2 1/4 cups (285g) all-purpose flour
- 1/2 teaspoon baking powder
- 1/4 teaspoon salt

For Taro Paste (if making your own):

- 1 medium taro root (about 8 oz, 225g), peeled and cubed
- 1/4 cup (50g) granulated sugar
- 1/4 cup (60ml) water
- Optional: 1 tablespoon unsalted butter

Instructions:

1. **Prepare Taro Paste:**
    - If making your own taro paste, steam or boil the taro cubes until tender, about 15-20 minutes. Drain and mash until smooth. Combine the mashed taro with granulated sugar and water in a saucepan over medium heat. Cook, stirring frequently, until the mixture thickens and becomes smooth. Stir in the butter if using. Allow the taro paste to cool before using.
2. **Preheat Oven:**
    - Preheat your oven to 350°F (175°C) and line a baking sheet with parchment paper.
3. **Cream Butter and Sugar:**
    - In a large bowl, cream together the softened butter and granulated sugar until light and fluffy.
4. **Add Egg and Vanilla:**
    - Beat in the egg and vanilla extract until well combined.
5. **Incorporate Taro Paste:**
    - Mix in the taro paste until fully combined with the butter and sugar mixture.
6. **Mix Dry Ingredients:**
    - In a separate bowl, whisk together the flour, baking powder, and salt.
7. **Combine Ingredients:**
    - Gradually add the dry ingredients to the wet mixture, mixing until just combined.
8. **Shape Cookies:**

- Scoop tablespoon-sized portions of dough and roll them into balls. Place them on the prepared baking sheet, spacing them about 2 inches apart. Flatten each ball slightly with the back of a spoon or your fingers.

9. **Bake:**
   - Bake in the preheated oven for 10-12 minutes, or until the edges are lightly golden. The centers may still be soft but will firm up as they cool.
10. **Cool:**
    - Allow the cookies to cool on the baking sheet for a few minutes before transferring them to a wire rack to cool completely.

Tips:

- **Taro Paste:** You can find taro paste in Asian grocery stores or online. It is often sweetened and ready to use, making it convenient.
- **Texture:** If the dough is too soft or sticky, chill it in the refrigerator for about 30 minutes before baking.
- **Storage:** Store the cookies in an airtight container at room temperature for up to a week. They can also be frozen for longer storage.

Taro cookies have a unique, subtly sweet flavor with a lovely purple hue, making them both visually appealing and delicious!

Kabocha Squash Cookies

Ingredients:

- 1 cup (1 stick, 115g) unsalted butter, softened
- 1 cup (200g) granulated sugar
- 1/2 cup (100g) packed brown sugar
- 1 large egg
- 1 cup (240g) cooked and mashed kabocha squash (see instructions below for preparation)
- 1 teaspoon vanilla extract
- 2 1/4 cups (285g) all-purpose flour
- 1 teaspoon baking powder
- 1/2 teaspoon baking soda
- 1/2 teaspoon ground cinnamon
- 1/4 teaspoon ground nutmeg
- 1/4 teaspoon salt

For Rolling (Optional):

- 1/4 cup (50g) granulated sugar
- 1 teaspoon ground cinnamon

Instructions:

1. **Prepare Kabocha Squash:**
   - Preheat your oven to 400°F (200°C). Cut the kabocha squash in half and remove the seeds. Place the halves cut-side down on a baking sheet and roast for 40-50 minutes, or until tender. Scoop out the flesh and mash until smooth. Allow to cool before using.
2. **Preheat Oven:**
   - Preheat your oven to 350°F (175°C) and line a baking sheet with parchment paper.
3. **Cream Butter and Sugars:**
   - In a large bowl, cream together the softened butter, granulated sugar, and brown sugar until light and fluffy.
4. **Add Egg, Kabocha, and Vanilla:**
   - Beat in the egg until well combined. Mix in the mashed kabocha squash and vanilla extract until smooth.
5. **Mix Dry Ingredients:**
   - In a separate bowl, whisk together the flour, baking powder, baking soda, cinnamon, nutmeg, and salt.
6. **Combine Ingredients:**

- Gradually add the dry ingredients to the wet mixture, mixing until just combined. The dough will be soft.
7. **Shape Cookies:**
    - If desired, mix the granulated sugar and ground cinnamon for rolling. Scoop tablespoon-sized portions of dough and roll them into balls. Roll each ball in the cinnamon-sugar mixture, if using, and place them on the prepared baking sheet, spacing them about 2 inches apart. Flatten each ball slightly with the back of a spoon or your fingers.
8. **Bake:**
    - Bake in the preheated oven for 10-12 minutes, or until the edges are lightly golden. The centers should be soft but set.
9. **Cool:**
    - Allow the cookies to cool on the baking sheet for a few minutes before transferring them to a wire rack to cool completely.

Tips:

- **Kabocha Squash:** If you don't have kabocha squash, you can use other types of winter squash like butternut squash or pumpkin, though the flavor will vary slightly.
- **Dough Consistency:** If the dough is too soft to handle, chill it in the refrigerator for about 30 minutes before baking.
- **Storage:** Store the cookies in an airtight container at room temperature for up to a week. They can also be frozen for longer storage.

These kabocha squash cookies offer a unique and flavorful twist on traditional cookies, perfect for fall or any time you're craving a sweet and cozy treat!

Sesame Almond Cookies

Ingredients:

- **1 cup (2 sticks, 230g) unsalted butter, softened**
- **3/4 cup (150g) granulated sugar**
- **1/2 cup (100g) brown sugar, packed**
- **1 large egg**
- **1 teaspoon vanilla extract**
- **1 cup (100g) finely chopped almonds** (or almond meal for a finer texture)
- **1 1/2 cups (190g) all-purpose flour**
- **1/2 teaspoon baking powder**
- **1/4 teaspoon salt**
- **1/2 cup (70g) sesame seeds** (for rolling and adding texture)

Instructions:

1. **Preheat Oven:**
   - Preheat your oven to 350°F (175°C) and line a baking sheet with parchment paper.
2. **Cream Butter and Sugars:**
   - In a large bowl, cream together the softened butter, granulated sugar, and brown sugar until light and fluffy.
3. **Add Egg and Vanilla:**
   - Beat in the egg and vanilla extract until well combined.
4. **Mix Dry Ingredients:**
   - In a separate bowl, whisk together the flour, baking powder, and salt.
5. **Combine Ingredients:**
   - Gradually add the dry ingredients to the wet mixture, mixing until just combined. Fold in the finely chopped almonds.
6. **Shape Cookies:**
   - Scoop tablespoon-sized portions of dough and roll them into balls. Roll each ball in the sesame seeds to coat the outside. Place the coated dough balls on the prepared baking sheet, spacing them about 2 inches apart. Flatten each ball slightly with the back of a spoon or your fingers.
7. **Bake:**
   - Bake in the preheated oven for 10-12 minutes, or until the edges are lightly golden. The centers should be soft but set.
8. **Cool:**
   - Allow the cookies to cool on the baking sheet for a few minutes before transferring them to a wire rack to cool completely.

Tips:

- **Almonds:** For a finer texture, you can use almond meal instead of chopped almonds. If using whole almonds, finely chop them to avoid large chunks in the cookies.
- **Sesame Seeds:** Toasting the sesame seeds lightly before using can enhance their flavor.
- **Dough Consistency:** If the dough is too soft to handle, chill it in the refrigerator for about 30 minutes before rolling and baking.
- **Storage:** Store the cookies in an airtight container at room temperature for up to a week. They can also be frozen for longer storage.

These sesame almond cookies offer a wonderful combination of crunchy sesame seeds and rich almond flavor, making them a perfect snack or dessert!

Uji Matcha Biscotti

Ingredients:

- 2 1/2 cups (315g) all-purpose flour
- 1 cup (200g) granulated sugar
- 1/2 cup (115g) unsalted butter, softened
- 3 large eggs
- 1/2 cup (70g) whole almonds (toasted or raw)
- 1 tablespoon Uji matcha powder (high-quality)
- 1 teaspoon baking powder
- 1/4 teaspoon salt
- 1 teaspoon vanilla extract

Optional Glaze:

- 1/2 cup (60g) powdered sugar
- 1-2 tablespoons water or milk
- 1 teaspoon Uji matcha powder

Instructions:

1. **Preheat Oven:**
   - Preheat your oven to 350°F (175°C). Line a baking sheet with parchment paper.
2. **Mix Dry Ingredients:**
   - In a bowl, whisk together the flour, Uji matcha powder, baking powder, and salt.
3. **Cream Butter and Sugar:**
   - In a large bowl, cream together the softened butter and granulated sugar until light and fluffy.
4. **Add Eggs and Vanilla:**
   - Beat in the eggs, one at a time, until well combined. Mix in the vanilla extract.
5. **Combine Ingredients:**
   - Gradually add the dry ingredients to the wet mixture, mixing until just combined. Fold in the whole almonds.
6. **Shape Dough:**
   - Divide the dough into two equal portions. Shape each portion into a log about 12 inches (30 cm) long and 2 inches (5 cm) wide, placing them on the prepared baking sheet. Flatten the logs slightly with your hands.
7. **Bake First Bake:**
   - Bake in the preheated oven for 25-30 minutes, or until the logs are firm and lightly golden. Remove from the oven and let cool on a wire rack for about 15 minutes.
8. **Slice and Second Bake:**

- Once the logs are cool enough to handle, transfer them to a cutting board and slice them diagonally into 1/2-inch (1.5 cm) thick pieces. Arrange the slices cut-side down on the baking sheet.
- Return the slices to the oven and bake for an additional 10-15 minutes, or until crisp and golden brown. Let cool completely on a wire rack.

9. **Prepare Glaze (Optional):**
   - If using the glaze, whisk together the powdered sugar, water or milk, and matcha powder until smooth. Drizzle over the cooled biscotti or dip the ends in the glaze and allow to set.

Tips:

- **Matcha Quality:** Use high-quality Uji matcha for the best flavor. It has a rich, vibrant taste that really shines in these biscotti.
- **Almonds:** Toast the almonds lightly before adding to the dough to enhance their flavor.
- **Storage:** Store the biscotti in an airtight container at room temperature for up to two weeks. They also freeze well for longer storage.

These Uji matcha biscotti are a perfect blend of Japanese and Italian flavors, offering a crunchy, flavorful treat that pairs wonderfully with tea or coffee!

Kinako (Roasted Soy Flour) Cookies

Ingredients:

- 1 cup (2 sticks, 230g) unsalted butter, softened
- 1 cup (200g) granulated sugar
- 1 large egg
- 1 teaspoon vanilla extract
- 1 cup (120g) kinako (roasted soy flour)
- 1 1/2 cups (190g) all-purpose flour
- 1/2 teaspoon baking powder
- 1/4 teaspoon salt

For Rolling (Optional):

- 1/4 cup (30g) granulated sugar mixed with 1 tablespoon kinako

Instructions:

1. **Preheat Oven:**
   - Preheat your oven to 350°F (175°C) and line a baking sheet with parchment paper.
2. **Cream Butter and Sugar:**
   - In a large bowl, cream together the softened butter and granulated sugar until light and fluffy.
3. **Add Egg and Vanilla:**
   - Beat in the egg and vanilla extract until well combined.
4. **Incorporate Kinako:**
   - Mix in the kinako until fully combined.
5. **Mix Dry Ingredients:**
   - In a separate bowl, whisk together the all-purpose flour, baking powder, and salt.
6. **Combine Ingredients:**
   - Gradually add the dry ingredients to the wet mixture, mixing until just combined. The dough will be slightly crumbly.
7. **Shape Cookies:**
   - Scoop tablespoon-sized portions of dough and roll them into balls. If desired, roll each ball in the sugar and kinako mixture for added flavor and texture. Place them on the prepared baking sheet, spacing them about 2 inches apart. Flatten each ball slightly with the back of a spoon or your fingers.
8. **Bake:**
   - Bake in the preheated oven for 10-12 minutes, or until the edges are lightly golden. The centers may still be soft but will firm up as they cool.
9. **Cool:**

- Allow the cookies to cool on the baking sheet for a few minutes before transferring them to a wire rack to cool completely.

Tips:

- **Kinako:** Kinako can be found at Asian grocery stores or online. If you don't have kinako, you can use roasted sesame seeds as an alternative, though the flavor will differ.
- **Texture:** The dough may seem a bit crumbly due to the kinako. If it's too dry, you can add a teaspoon of milk to help bind it.
- **Storage:** Store the cookies in an airtight container at room temperature for up to a week. They can also be frozen for longer storage.

These kinako cookies offer a distinctive nutty flavor and a delightful texture, making them a unique and enjoyable treat!

Japanese Cheesecake Cookies

Ingredients:

- 1 cup (2 sticks, 230g) unsalted butter, softened
- 1 cup (200g) granulated sugar
- 1/2 cup (100g) cream cheese, softened
- 1 large egg
- 1 teaspoon vanilla extract
- 2 cups (250g) all-purpose flour
- 1/2 teaspoon baking powder
- 1/4 teaspoon salt

For Optional Topping:

- Powdered sugar for dusting

Instructions:

1. **Preheat Oven:**
   - Preheat your oven to 350°F (175°C) and line a baking sheet with parchment paper.
2. **Cream Butter, Sugar, and Cream Cheese:**
   - In a large bowl, cream together the softened butter, granulated sugar, and cream cheese until light and fluffy.
3. **Add Egg and Vanilla:**
   - Beat in the egg and vanilla extract until well combined.
4. **Mix Dry Ingredients:**
   - In a separate bowl, whisk together the flour, baking powder, and salt.
5. **Combine Ingredients:**
   - Gradually add the dry ingredients to the wet mixture, mixing until just combined. The dough will be soft but manageable.
6. **Shape Cookies:**
   - Scoop tablespoon-sized portions of dough and place them on the prepared baking sheet, spacing them about 2 inches apart. Flatten each dough ball slightly with the back of a spoon or your fingers.
7. **Bake:**
   - Bake in the preheated oven for 10-12 minutes, or until the edges are lightly golden. The centers should remain soft.
8. **Cool:**
   - Allow the cookies to cool on the baking sheet for a few minutes before transferring them to a wire rack to cool completely.
9. **Dust with Powdered Sugar (Optional):**

- Once cooled, you can dust the cookies with powdered sugar for a touch of sweetness and presentation.

Tips:

- **Cream Cheese:** Make sure the cream cheese is fully softened for a smooth and creamy texture in the dough.
- **Texture:** These cookies are meant to be soft and slightly chewy, similar to the texture of Japanese cheesecake. If you prefer a firmer cookie, you can chill the dough before baking.
- **Storage:** Store the cookies in an airtight container at room temperature for up to a week. They can also be frozen for longer storage.

Japanese cheesecake cookies offer a wonderful combination of creamy and fluffy textures, perfect for enjoying with tea or as a special treat!

Mochi Cookies

Ingredients:

- 1 cup (2 sticks, 230g) unsalted butter, softened
- 1 cup (200g) granulated sugar
- 1/2 cup (100g) packed brown sugar
- 1 large egg
- 1 teaspoon vanilla extract
- 1 cup (120g) mochiko (sweet rice flour)
- 1 cup (130g) all-purpose flour
- 1/2 teaspoon baking powder
- 1/4 teaspoon salt
- 1/2 cup (85g) white chocolate chips or chopped chocolate (optional)
- 1/4 cup (30g) toasted sesame seeds (optional)

For Rolling (Optional):

- 1/4 cup (30g) granulated sugar mixed with 1 teaspoon ground cinnamon

Instructions:

1. **Preheat Oven:**
    - Preheat your oven to 350°F (175°C) and line a baking sheet with parchment paper.
2. **Cream Butter and Sugars:**
    - In a large bowl, cream together the softened butter, granulated sugar, and brown sugar until light and fluffy.
3. **Add Egg and Vanilla:**
    - Beat in the egg and vanilla extract until well combined.
4. **Mix Dry Ingredients:**
    - In a separate bowl, whisk together the mochiko, all-purpose flour, baking powder, and salt.
5. **Combine Ingredients:**
    - Gradually add the dry ingredients to the wet mixture, mixing until just combined. If using, fold in the white chocolate chips or chopped chocolate and toasted sesame seeds.
6. **Shape Cookies:**
    - Scoop tablespoon-sized portions of dough and roll them into balls. If desired, roll each ball in the sugar and cinnamon mixture before placing them on the prepared baking sheet, spacing them about 2 inches apart. Flatten each ball slightly with the back of a spoon or your fingers.
7. **Bake:**

- - Bake in the preheated oven for 10-12 minutes, or until the edges are lightly golden. The centers should remain soft and chewy.
8. **Cool:**
    - Allow the cookies to cool on the baking sheet for a few minutes before transferring them to a wire rack to cool completely.

Tips:

- **Mochiko:** Mochiko is a type of sweet rice flour used to make mochi. It can be found in Asian grocery stores or online.
- **Texture:** The cookies should have a chewy texture due to the mochiko. If the dough is too soft, you can chill it in the refrigerator for about 30 minutes before baking.
- **Storage:** Store the cookies in an airtight container at room temperature for up to a week. They can also be frozen for longer storage.

These mochi cookies combine the best of both worlds—chewy mochi texture and sweet, buttery cookie flavor—making them a unique and delicious treat!

Japanese Sweet Potato and Nut Cookies

Ingredients:

- 1 cup (2 sticks, 230g) unsalted butter, softened
- 1 cup (200g) granulated sugar
- 1/2 cup (100g) packed brown sugar
- 1 large egg
- 1 teaspoon vanilla extract
- 1 cup (200g) cooked and mashed Japanese sweet potato (see instructions below for preparation)
- 2 1/4 cups (285g) all-purpose flour
- 1 teaspoon baking powder
- 1/4 teaspoon salt
- 1/2 cup (70g) chopped nuts (such as walnuts, pecans, or almonds)
- 1/4 teaspoon ground cinnamon (optional)

For Rolling (Optional):

- 1/4 cup (30g) granulated sugar mixed with 1 teaspoon ground cinnamon

Instructions:

1. **Prepare Sweet Potato:**
   - Preheat your oven to 400°F (200°C). Cut the sweet potato into chunks and roast or bake it for about 40-50 minutes, or until tender. Let it cool, then peel and mash until smooth. Measure out 1 cup of mashed sweet potato.
2. **Preheat Oven:**
   - Preheat your oven to 350°F (175°C) and line a baking sheet with parchment paper.
3. **Cream Butter and Sugars:**
   - In a large bowl, cream together the softened butter, granulated sugar, and brown sugar until light and fluffy.
4. **Add Egg, Vanilla, and Sweet Potato:**
   - Beat in the egg and vanilla extract until well combined. Mix in the mashed sweet potato until smooth.
5. **Mix Dry Ingredients:**
   - In a separate bowl, whisk together the flour, baking powder, salt, and ground cinnamon (if using).
6. **Combine Ingredients:**
   - Gradually add the dry ingredients to the wet mixture, mixing until just combined. Fold in the chopped nuts.
7. **Shape Cookies:**

- Scoop tablespoon-sized portions of dough and roll them into balls. If desired, roll each ball in the sugar and cinnamon mixture before placing them on the prepared baking sheet, spacing them about 2 inches apart. Flatten each ball slightly with the back of a spoon or your fingers.

8. **Bake:**
   - Bake in the preheated oven for 10-12 minutes, or until the edges are lightly golden. The centers should be soft but set.
9. **Cool:**
   - Allow the cookies to cool on the baking sheet for a few minutes before transferring them to a wire rack to cool completely.

Tips:

- **Sweet Potato:** Japanese sweet potatoes are sweeter and have a richer flavor compared to regular sweet potatoes. If you can't find them, you can use regular sweet potatoes or even canned sweet potato puree.
- **Nuts:** Toast the nuts lightly before chopping and adding to the dough to enhance their flavor.
- **Texture:** The dough might be a bit soft due to the mashed sweet potato. If it's too sticky, chill the dough in the refrigerator for about 30 minutes before shaping and baking.
- **Storage:** Store the cookies in an airtight container at room temperature for up to a week. They can also be frozen for longer storage.

These Japanese sweet potato and nut cookies are a delightful combination of sweet, nutty, and creamy flavors, making them a perfect treat for any occasion!

Yatsuhashi Cookies

Ingredients:

- **1 cup (2 sticks, 230g) unsalted butter, softened**
- **1 cup (200g) granulated sugar**
- **1 large egg**
- **1 teaspoon vanilla extract**
- **1 cup (120g) mochiko (sweet rice flour)**
- **1 1/2 cups (190g) all-purpose flour**
- **1/2 teaspoon baking powder**
- **1/4 teaspoon salt**
- **1 teaspoon ground cinnamon** (or more if you like a stronger flavor, or you can substitute with matcha powder for a different flavor)
- **1/4 cup (40g) chopped nuts** (optional, such as walnuts or almonds)

For Optional Glaze:

- **1/2 cup (60g) powdered sugar**
- **1-2 tablespoons water or milk**
- **1/2 teaspoon ground cinnamon** (if making a cinnamon glaze) or **1 teaspoon matcha powder** (if making a matcha glaze)

Instructions:

1. **Preheat Oven:**
   - Preheat your oven to 350°F (175°C) and line a baking sheet with parchment paper.
2. **Cream Butter and Sugar:**
   - In a large bowl, cream together the softened butter and granulated sugar until light and fluffy.
3. **Add Egg and Vanilla:**
   - Beat in the egg and vanilla extract until well combined.
4. **Mix Dry Ingredients:**
   - In a separate bowl, whisk together the mochiko, all-purpose flour, baking powder, salt, and ground cinnamon.
5. **Combine Ingredients:**
   - Gradually add the dry ingredients to the wet mixture, mixing until just combined. If using, fold in the chopped nuts.
6. **Shape Cookies:**
   - Scoop tablespoon-sized portions of dough and roll them into balls. Place them on the prepared baking sheet, spacing them about 2 inches apart. Flatten each ball slightly with the back of a spoon or your fingers.

7. **Bake:**
   - Bake in the preheated oven for 10-12 minutes, or until the edges are lightly golden. The centers should be soft but set.
8. **Cool:**
   - Allow the cookies to cool on the baking sheet for a few minutes before transferring them to a wire rack to cool completely.
9. **Prepare Glaze (Optional):**
   - If using the glaze, whisk together the powdered sugar with water or milk and cinnamon or matcha powder until smooth. Drizzle or dip the cookies in the glaze and let set.

Tips:

- **Mochiko:** Mochiko is essential for achieving the chewy texture reminiscent of Yatsuhashi. It's available at Asian grocery stores or online.
- **Flavor Variations:** You can adjust the flavor by using matcha powder instead of cinnamon, or even adding other spices or flavor extracts to taste.
- **Texture:** The cookies should be soft and slightly chewy. If the dough is too sticky, chill it in the refrigerator for about 30 minutes before baking.
- **Storage:** Store the cookies in an airtight container at room temperature for up to a week. They can also be frozen for longer storage.

These Yatsuhashi-inspired cookies offer a delightful twist on a traditional Japanese treat, blending the chewy, sweet essence of Yatsuhashi with the convenience of cookies!

Soy Sauce Caramel Cookies

Ingredients:

- **1 cup (2 sticks, 230g) unsalted butter, softened**
- **1 cup (200g) granulated sugar**
- **1/2 cup (100g) packed brown sugar**
- **1/2 cup (120g) caramel sauce** (store-bought or homemade)
- **1 tablespoon soy sauce** (use a good quality soy sauce for best results)
- **1 large egg**
- **1 teaspoon vanilla extract**
- **2 1/4 cups (285g) all-purpose flour**
- **1 teaspoon baking powder**
- **1/2 teaspoon baking soda**
- **1/4 teaspoon salt**

Optional Topping:

- **Coarse sea salt for sprinkling**

Instructions:

1. **Preheat Oven:**
   - Preheat your oven to 350°F (175°C) and line a baking sheet with parchment paper.
2. **Cream Butter and Sugars:**
   - In a large bowl, cream together the softened butter, granulated sugar, and brown sugar until light and fluffy.
3. **Add Caramel, Soy Sauce, Egg, and Vanilla:**
   - Mix in the caramel sauce and soy sauce until well combined. Beat in the egg and vanilla extract until smooth.
4. **Mix Dry Ingredients:**
   - In a separate bowl, whisk together the flour, baking powder, baking soda, and salt.
5. **Combine Ingredients:**
   - Gradually add the dry ingredients to the wet mixture, mixing until just combined. The dough will be soft.
6. **Shape Cookies:**
   - Scoop tablespoon-sized portions of dough and place them on the prepared baking sheet, spacing them about 2 inches apart. Flatten each dough ball slightly with the back of a spoon or your fingers.
7. **Optional Topping:**

- If desired, sprinkle a pinch of coarse sea salt on top of each cookie before baking for an extra touch of flavor.
8. **Bake:**
    - Bake in the preheated oven for 10-12 minutes, or until the edges are golden and the centers are set. The cookies will continue to firm up as they cool.
9. **Cool:**
    - Allow the cookies to cool on the baking sheet for a few minutes before transferring them to a wire rack to cool completely.

Tips:

- **Caramel Sauce:** Use a high-quality caramel sauce for the best flavor. If using homemade caramel sauce, make sure it's cooled and thickened before incorporating it into the dough.
- **Soy Sauce:** A small amount of soy sauce adds a unique umami flavor that complements the caramel. Ensure that it is well mixed into the dough.
- **Texture:** The cookies will be slightly chewy with a rich, caramel flavor. If the dough is too soft to handle, chill it in the refrigerator for about 30 minutes before baking.
- **Storage:** Store the cookies in an airtight container at room temperature for up to a week. They can also be frozen for longer storage.

These soy sauce caramel cookies offer an intriguing blend of sweet, salty, and savory flavors, making them a memorable treat for any cookie lover!

Plum Wine Cookies

Ingredients:

- 1 cup (2 sticks, 230g) unsalted butter, softened
- 1 cup (200g) granulated sugar
- 1/2 cup (100g) packed brown sugar
- 1 large egg
- 1 teaspoon vanilla extract
- 1/4 cup (60ml) plum wine (such as Umeshu or any sweet plum wine)
- 2 1/4 cups (285g) all-purpose flour
- 1/2 teaspoon baking powder
- 1/4 teaspoon baking soda
- 1/4 teaspoon salt

Optional Glaze:

- 1/2 cup (60g) powdered sugar
- 1-2 tablespoons plum wine (adjust for consistency)

Instructions:

1. **Preheat Oven:**
   - Preheat your oven to 350°F (175°C) and line a baking sheet with parchment paper.
2. **Cream Butter and Sugars:**
   - In a large bowl, cream together the softened butter, granulated sugar, and brown sugar until light and fluffy.
3. **Add Egg, Vanilla, and Plum Wine:**
   - Beat in the egg and vanilla extract until well combined. Mix in the plum wine until smooth.
4. **Mix Dry Ingredients:**
   - In a separate bowl, whisk together the flour, baking powder, baking soda, and salt.
5. **Combine Ingredients:**
   - Gradually add the dry ingredients to the wet mixture, mixing until just combined. The dough will be soft.
6. **Shape Cookies:**
   - Scoop tablespoon-sized portions of dough and place them on the prepared baking sheet, spacing them about 2 inches apart. Flatten each ball slightly with the back of a spoon or your fingers.
7. **Bake:**

- Bake in the preheated oven for 10-12 minutes, or until the edges are lightly golden. The centers should remain soft.
8. **Cool:**
   - Allow the cookies to cool on the baking sheet for a few minutes before transferring them to a wire rack to cool completely.
9. **Prepare Glaze (Optional):**
   - If using the glaze, whisk together the powdered sugar and plum wine until smooth and drizzle over the cooled cookies.

Tips:

- **Plum Wine:** Use a sweet plum wine (umeshu) for a richer flavor. If you can't find plum wine, you can use another sweet liqueur or even a fruit juice, though the flavor will vary.
- **Texture:** The cookies should be soft with a subtle fruity flavor. If the dough is too sticky, chill it in the refrigerator for about 30 minutes before baking.
- **Glaze:** The glaze is optional but adds a nice finishing touch and enhances the plum flavor. Adjust the amount of plum wine in the glaze to achieve the desired consistency.

These plum wine cookies offer a unique and sophisticated flavor profile, making them a special treat for any occasion!

Choco-Banana Mochi Cookies

Ingredients:

- 1 cup (2 sticks, 230g) unsalted butter, softened
- 1 cup (200g) granulated sugar
- 1/2 cup (100g) packed brown sugar
- 1 large egg
- 1 teaspoon vanilla extract
- 1/2 cup (120g) mashed ripe banana (about 1 medium banana)
- 1 cup (120g) mochiko (sweet rice flour)
- 1 1/2 cups (190g) all-purpose flour
- 1/2 teaspoon baking powder
- 1/4 teaspoon baking soda
- 1/4 teaspoon salt
- 1 cup (170g) semi-sweet chocolate chips or chunks

Optional Topping:

- 1/4 cup (30g) granulated sugar mixed with 1 teaspoon ground cinnamon (for rolling before baking)

Instructions:

1. **Preheat Oven:**
   - Preheat your oven to 350°F (175°C) and line a baking sheet with parchment paper.
2. **Cream Butter and Sugars:**
   - In a large bowl, cream together the softened butter, granulated sugar, and brown sugar until light and fluffy.
3. **Add Egg, Vanilla, and Banana:**
   - Beat in the egg and vanilla extract until well combined. Mix in the mashed banana until smooth.
4. **Mix Dry Ingredients:**
   - In a separate bowl, whisk together the mochiko, all-purpose flour, baking powder, baking soda, and salt.
5. **Combine Ingredients:**
   - Gradually add the dry ingredients to the wet mixture, mixing until just combined. Fold in the chocolate chips or chunks.
6. **Shape Cookies:**
   - Scoop tablespoon-sized portions of dough and roll them into balls. If desired, roll each ball in the sugar and cinnamon mixture before placing them on the prepared

baking sheet, spacing them about 2 inches apart. Flatten each ball slightly with the back of a spoon or your fingers.
7. **Bake:**
    - Bake in the preheated oven for 10-12 minutes, or until the edges are lightly golden. The centers should remain soft and chewy.
8. **Cool:**
    - Allow the cookies to cool on the baking sheet for a few minutes before transferring them to a wire rack to cool completely.

Tips:

- **Banana:** Use ripe bananas for the best flavor and sweetness. Make sure the banana is well-mashed to ensure even distribution in the dough.
- **Mochiko:** Mochiko (sweet rice flour) gives the cookies their chewy texture. It's available at Asian grocery stores or online.
- **Texture:** The cookies will have a soft, chewy texture due to the mochiko. If the dough is too soft to handle, you can chill it in the refrigerator for about 30 minutes before baking.
- **Storage:** Store the cookies in an airtight container at room temperature for up to a week. They can also be frozen for longer storage.

These choco-banana mochi cookies offer a wonderful combination of chewy mochi, sweet banana, and rich chocolate, making them a unique and delicious treat!

Azuki Bean and Walnut Cookies

Ingredients:

- 1 cup (2 sticks, 230g) unsalted butter, softened
- 1 cup (200g) granulated sugar
- 1/2 cup (100g) packed brown sugar
- 1 large egg
- 1 teaspoon vanilla extract
- 1/2 cup (120g) smooth azuki bean paste (anko, store-bought or homemade; see notes below for making your own)
- 1 1/2 cups (190g) all-purpose flour
- 1/2 teaspoon baking powder
- 1/4 teaspoon baking soda
- 1/4 teaspoon salt
- 1/2 cup (70g) chopped walnuts

For Optional Topping:

- 1/4 cup (30g) granulated sugar mixed with 1/2 teaspoon ground cinnamon

Instructions:

1. **Preheat Oven:**
   - Preheat your oven to 350°F (175°C) and line a baking sheet with parchment paper.
2. **Cream Butter and Sugars:**
   - In a large bowl, cream together the softened butter, granulated sugar, and brown sugar until light and fluffy.
3. **Add Egg, Vanilla, and Azuki Bean Paste:**
   - Beat in the egg and vanilla extract until well combined. Mix in the azuki bean paste until smooth and fully incorporated.
4. **Mix Dry Ingredients:**
   - In a separate bowl, whisk together the flour, baking powder, baking soda, and salt.
5. **Combine Ingredients:**
   - Gradually add the dry ingredients to the wet mixture, mixing until just combined. Fold in the chopped walnuts.
6. **Shape Cookies:**
   - Scoop tablespoon-sized portions of dough and roll them into balls. If desired, roll each ball in the sugar and cinnamon mixture before placing them on the prepared baking sheet, spacing them about 2 inches apart. Flatten each ball slightly with the back of a spoon or your fingers.

7. **Bake:**
   - Bake in the preheated oven for 10-12 minutes, or until the edges are lightly golden. The centers should remain soft but set.
8. **Cool:**
   - Allow the cookies to cool on the baking sheet for a few minutes before transferring them to a wire rack to cool completely.

Notes:

- **Azuki Bean Paste:** You can find smooth azuki bean paste (anko) at Asian grocery stores or online. If you want to make your own, cook 1 cup of dried azuki beans with 1 cup of sugar and water until tender, then mash or blend until smooth.
- **Texture:** The azuki bean paste adds moisture and a unique flavor to the cookies. The dough might be slightly softer due to the paste, so chilling the dough for about 30 minutes before baking can help if the dough is too sticky to handle.
- **Nuts:** Toast the walnuts lightly before chopping and adding to the dough to enhance their flavor.
- **Storage:** Store the cookies in an airtight container at room temperature for up to a week. They can also be frozen for longer storage.

These azuki bean and walnut cookies offer a delightful combination of sweet and nutty flavors with a chewy texture, making them a unique and enjoyable treat!

Green Tea and White Chocolate Cookies

Ingredients:

- 1 cup (2 sticks, 230g) unsalted butter, softened
- 1 cup (200g) granulated sugar
- 1/2 cup (100g) packed brown sugar
- 1 large egg
- 1 teaspoon vanilla extract
- 1 1/2 cups (180g) all-purpose flour
- 1 cup (120g) mochiko (sweet rice flour) (optional for a chewier texture)
- 1 tablespoon matcha green tea powder (culinary grade)
- 1/2 teaspoon baking powder
- 1/4 teaspoon baking soda
- 1/4 teaspoon salt
- 1 cup (170g) white chocolate chips or chopped white chocolate

Optional Topping:

- Additional matcha powder for sprinkling

Instructions:

1. **Preheat Oven:**
   - Preheat your oven to 350°F (175°C) and line a baking sheet with parchment paper.
2. **Cream Butter and Sugars:**
   - In a large bowl, cream together the softened butter, granulated sugar, and brown sugar until light and fluffy.
3. **Add Egg and Vanilla:**
   - Beat in the egg and vanilla extract until well combined.
4. **Mix Dry Ingredients:**
   - In a separate bowl, whisk together the flour, mochiko (if using), matcha powder, baking powder, baking soda, and salt.
5. **Combine Ingredients:**
   - Gradually add the dry ingredients to the wet mixture, mixing until just combined. Fold in the white chocolate chips or chunks.
6. **Shape Cookies:**
   - Scoop tablespoon-sized portions of dough and place them on the prepared baking sheet, spacing them about 2 inches apart. Flatten each ball slightly with the back of a spoon or your fingers.
7. **Bake:**

        - Bake in the preheated oven for 10-12 minutes, or until the edges are lightly golden. The centers should remain soft and slightly underbaked for a chewy texture.
8. **Cool:**
    - Allow the cookies to cool on the baking sheet for a few minutes before transferring them to a wire rack to cool completely.
9. **Optional Topping:**
    - If desired, sprinkle a little additional matcha powder on top of the cookies while they are still warm for a pop of color and flavor.

Tips:

- **Matcha Powder:** Use high-quality culinary matcha powder for the best flavor and color. If you prefer a more intense green tea flavor, you can increase the amount of matcha powder slightly.
- **Mochiko:** Adding mochiko (sweet rice flour) gives the cookies a slightly chewier texture, but you can omit it if you prefer a more traditional cookie texture.
- **Texture:** The cookies should have a soft, chewy texture with a burst of white chocolate and a subtle matcha flavor. If the dough is too sticky, chill it in the refrigerator for about 30 minutes before baking.
- **Storage:** Store the cookies in an airtight container at room temperature for up to a week. They can also be frozen for longer storage.

These green tea and white chocolate cookies are a sophisticated treat that combines the best of both worlds—creamy white chocolate and vibrant green tea flavor!

Shiso Leaf Cookies

Ingredients:

- 1 cup (2 sticks, 230g) unsalted butter, softened
- 1 cup (200g) granulated sugar
- 1/2 cup (100g) packed brown sugar
- 1 large egg
- 1 teaspoon vanilla extract
- 1 1/2 cups (190g) all-purpose flour
- 1/2 cup (60g) cornstarch
- 1 teaspoon baking powder
- 1/4 teaspoon salt
- 1/4 cup finely chopped fresh shiso leaves (about 10-15 leaves, or to taste)
- Optional: 1/4 cup granulated sugar for rolling

Instructions:

1. **Prepare Shiso Leaves:**
   - Wash and thoroughly dry the shiso leaves. Stack them and cut into thin strips or finely chop them. Set aside.
2. **Preheat Oven:**
   - Preheat your oven to 350°F (175°C) and line a baking sheet with parchment paper.
3. **Cream Butter and Sugars:**
   - In a large bowl, cream together the softened butter, granulated sugar, and brown sugar until light and fluffy.
4. **Add Egg and Vanilla:**
   - Beat in the egg and vanilla extract until well combined.
5. **Mix Dry Ingredients:**
   - In a separate bowl, whisk together the flour, cornstarch, baking powder, and salt.
6. **Combine Ingredients:**
   - Gradually add the dry ingredients to the wet mixture, mixing until just combined. Gently fold in the finely chopped shiso leaves.
7. **Shape Cookies:**
   - Scoop tablespoon-sized portions of dough and roll them into balls. If desired, roll each ball in granulated sugar before placing them on the prepared baking sheet, spacing them about 2 inches apart. Flatten each ball slightly with the back of a spoon or your fingers.
8. **Bake:**
   - Bake in the preheated oven for 10-12 minutes, or until the edges are lightly golden. The centers should be soft but set.
9. **Cool:**

- Allow the cookies to cool on the baking sheet for a few minutes before transferring them to a wire rack to cool completely.

Tips:

- **Shiso Leaves:** Use fresh shiso leaves for the best flavor. If shiso leaves are unavailable, you might experiment with other herbs like mint or basil, but the flavor will be different.
- **Cornstarch:** The cornstarch in the recipe helps create a tender texture. If you prefer a firmer cookie, you can reduce or omit the cornstarch.
- **Texture:** The cookies should have a delicate texture with a subtle herbal flavor from the shiso. If the dough is too soft, chill it in the refrigerator for about 30 minutes before baking.
- **Storage:** Store the cookies in an airtight container at room temperature for up to a week. They can also be frozen for longer storage.

These shiso leaf cookies offer a refreshing and unique twist on traditional cookies, showcasing the aromatic qualities of shiso in a sweet treat. Enjoy!

Chestnut and Maple Cookies

Ingredients:

- 1 cup (2 sticks, 230g) unsalted butter, softened
- 1 cup (200g) granulated sugar
- 1/2 cup (100g) packed brown sugar
- 1/2 cup (120ml) pure maple syrup
- 1 large egg
- 1 teaspoon vanilla extract
- 1 1/2 cups (190g) all-purpose flour
- 1/2 cup (60g) finely chopped cooked chestnuts (can use canned or roasted chestnuts, finely chopped or mashed)
- 1 teaspoon baking powder
- 1/4 teaspoon baking soda
- 1/4 teaspoon salt

Optional Glaze:

- 1/2 cup (60g) powdered sugar
- 1-2 tablespoons pure maple syrup

Instructions:

1. **Preheat Oven:**
   - Preheat your oven to 350°F (175°C) and line a baking sheet with parchment paper.
2. **Cream Butter and Sugars:**
   - In a large bowl, cream together the softened butter, granulated sugar, and brown sugar until light and fluffy.
3. **Add Maple Syrup, Egg, and Vanilla:**
   - Beat in the maple syrup, egg, and vanilla extract until well combined.
4. **Mix Dry Ingredients:**
   - In a separate bowl, whisk together the flour, baking powder, baking soda, and salt.
5. **Combine Ingredients:**
   - Gradually add the dry ingredients to the wet mixture, mixing until just combined. Fold in the finely chopped or mashed chestnuts.
6. **Shape Cookies:**
   - Scoop tablespoon-sized portions of dough and place them on the prepared baking sheet, spacing them about 2 inches apart. Flatten each ball slightly with the back of a spoon or your fingers.

7. **Bake:**
   - Bake in the preheated oven for 10-12 minutes, or until the edges are lightly golden and the centers are set. The cookies will firm up as they cool.
8. **Cool:**
   - Allow the cookies to cool on the baking sheet for a few minutes before transferring them to a wire rack to cool completely.
9. **Prepare Glaze (Optional):**
   - If using the glaze, whisk together the powdered sugar and maple syrup until smooth. Drizzle over the cooled cookies.

Tips:

- **Chestnuts:** Use cooked chestnuts for the best texture. You can use canned chestnuts, which are already cooked, or roast your own. Ensure they are finely chopped or mashed so they incorporate well into the cookie dough.
- **Maple Syrup:** Use pure maple syrup for the best flavor. Avoid imitation maple syrup, which can have a less refined taste.
- **Texture:** The cookies will be soft and slightly chewy with a rich chestnut and maple flavor. If the dough is too sticky, you can chill it in the refrigerator for about 30 minutes before baking.
- **Storage:** Store the cookies in an airtight container at room temperature for up to a week. They can also be frozen for longer storage.

These chestnut and maple cookies bring together two wonderful flavors in a delightful, sweet treat that's perfect for cozy gatherings or as a special treat during the colder months. Enjoy!

Wasabi and Sesame Cookies

Ingredients:

- 1 cup (2 sticks, 230g) unsalted butter, softened
- 1 cup (200g) granulated sugar
- 1/2 cup (100g) packed brown sugar
- 1 large egg
- 1 teaspoon vanilla extract
- 2 tablespoons wasabi paste (adjust based on heat preference)
- 1 1/2 cups (190g) all-purpose flour
- 1/2 cup (60g) sesame seeds (toasted or untoasted)
- 1/2 teaspoon baking powder
- 1/4 teaspoon baking soda
- 1/4 teaspoon salt

Optional Glaze:

- 1/4 cup (30g) powdered sugar
- 1-2 tablespoons milk or water

Instructions:

1. **Preheat Oven:**
   - Preheat your oven to 350°F (175°C) and line a baking sheet with parchment paper.
2. **Cream Butter and Sugars:**
   - In a large bowl, cream together the softened butter, granulated sugar, and brown sugar until light and fluffy.
3. **Add Egg, Vanilla, and Wasabi Paste:**
   - Beat in the egg and vanilla extract until well combined. Mix in the wasabi paste until fully incorporated. Adjust the amount of wasabi paste to your heat preference.
4. **Mix Dry Ingredients:**
   - In a separate bowl, whisk together the flour, baking powder, baking soda, and salt.
5. **Combine Ingredients:**
   - Gradually add the dry ingredients to the wet mixture, mixing until just combined. Fold in the sesame seeds.
6. **Shape Cookies:**
   - Scoop tablespoon-sized portions of dough and place them on the prepared baking sheet, spacing them about 2 inches apart. Flatten each ball slightly with the back of a spoon or your fingers.

7. **Bake:**
   - Bake in the preheated oven for 10-12 minutes, or until the edges are lightly golden. The centers should remain soft.
8. **Cool:**
   - Allow the cookies to cool on the baking sheet for a few minutes before transferring them to a wire rack to cool completely.
9. **Prepare Glaze (Optional):**
   - If using the glaze, whisk together the powdered sugar and milk or water until smooth. Drizzle over the cooled cookies for a touch of sweetness.

Tips:

- **Wasabi Paste:** Adjust the amount of wasabi paste according to your taste. Wasabi paste can vary in strength, so start with less if you're unsure and increase to taste.
- **Sesame Seeds:** Toasting the sesame seeds before adding them to the dough enhances their flavor, but raw sesame seeds will also work.
- **Texture:** These cookies will have a unique combination of sweet, savory, and spicy flavors with a chewy texture. If the dough is too soft, chill it in the refrigerator for about 30 minutes before baking.
- **Storage:** Store the cookies in an airtight container at room temperature for up to a week. They can also be frozen for longer storage.

These wasabi and sesame cookies offer a delightful balance of flavors and are perfect for those who enjoy a bit of spice in their sweets. They're a great way to surprise and delight your taste buds with something a little different!

Miso and Brown Sugar Cookies

Ingredients:

- 1 cup (2 sticks, 230g) unsalted butter, softened
- 1 cup (200g) packed brown sugar
- 1/2 cup (100g) granulated sugar
- 1/4 cup (60g) white miso paste (smooth or mellow miso for a subtler flavor)
- 1 large egg
- 1 teaspoon vanilla extract
- 2 1/4 cups (285g) all-purpose flour
- 1/2 teaspoon baking powder
- 1/4 teaspoon baking soda
- 1/4 teaspoon salt

Optional Glaze:

- 1/2 cup (60g) powdered sugar
- 1-2 tablespoons milk or water

Instructions:

1. **Preheat Oven:**
    - Preheat your oven to 350°F (175°C) and line a baking sheet with parchment paper.
2. **Cream Butter and Sugars:**
    - In a large bowl, cream together the softened butter, brown sugar, and granulated sugar until light and fluffy.
3. **Add Miso, Egg, and Vanilla:**
    - Beat in the miso paste until well combined. Then, add the egg and vanilla extract, mixing until fully incorporated.
4. **Mix Dry Ingredients:**
    - In a separate bowl, whisk together the flour, baking powder, baking soda, and salt.
5. **Combine Ingredients:**
    - Gradually add the dry ingredients to the wet mixture, mixing until just combined.
6. **Shape Cookies:**
    - Scoop tablespoon-sized portions of dough and place them on the prepared baking sheet, spacing them about 2 inches apart. Flatten each ball slightly with the back of a spoon or your fingers.
7. **Bake:**
    - Bake in the preheated oven for 10-12 minutes, or until the edges are lightly golden. The centers should remain soft.

8. **Cool:**
   - Allow the cookies to cool on the baking sheet for a few minutes before transferring them to a wire rack to cool completely.
9. **Prepare Glaze (Optional):**
   - If using the glaze, whisk together the powdered sugar and milk or water until smooth. Drizzle over the cooled cookies for a touch of sweetness.

Tips:

- **Miso Paste:** Use a smooth, light-colored miso (like white or mellow miso) for a subtler flavor. Darker misos can be more pungent and might overpower the sweetness.
- **Texture:** These cookies will have a soft, chewy texture with a unique sweet and savory flavor. If the dough seems too soft, chill it in the refrigerator for about 30 minutes before baking.
- **Flavor Balance:** The miso adds a savory umami flavor that complements the sweetness of the brown sugar. Adjust the amount of miso paste based on your taste preference.
- **Storage:** Store the cookies in an airtight container at room temperature for up to a week. They can also be frozen for longer storage.

These miso and brown sugar cookies offer an intriguing combination of sweet and savory flavors, making them a standout treat that's perfect for those who enjoy a unique twist on traditional cookies.

Sake-Infused Cookies

Ingredients:

- 1 cup (2 sticks, 230g) unsalted butter, softened
- 1 cup (200g) granulated sugar
- 1/2 cup (100g) packed brown sugar
- 1 large egg
- 1 teaspoon vanilla extract
- 1/4 cup (60ml) sake (preferably a smooth, slightly sweet sake)
- 2 1/4 cups (285g) all-purpose flour
- 1/2 teaspoon baking powder
- 1/4 teaspoon baking soda
- 1/4 teaspoon salt

Optional Glaze:

- 1/2 cup (60g) powdered sugar
- 1-2 tablespoons sake (to make a sake glaze)
- Zest of 1 lemon or orange (optional, for added flavor)

Instructions:

1. **Preheat Oven:**
   - Preheat your oven to 350°F (175°C) and line a baking sheet with parchment paper.
2. **Cream Butter and Sugars:**
   - In a large bowl, cream together the softened butter, granulated sugar, and brown sugar until light and fluffy.
3. **Add Egg, Vanilla, and Sake:**
   - Beat in the egg and vanilla extract until well combined. Mix in the sake until fully incorporated.
4. **Mix Dry Ingredients:**
   - In a separate bowl, whisk together the flour, baking powder, baking soda, and salt.
5. **Combine Ingredients:**
   - Gradually add the dry ingredients to the wet mixture, mixing until just combined.
6. **Shape Cookies:**
   - Scoop tablespoon-sized portions of dough and place them on the prepared baking sheet, spacing them about 2 inches apart. Flatten each ball slightly with the back of a spoon or your fingers.
7. **Bake:**

- Bake in the preheated oven for 10-12 minutes, or until the edges are lightly golden and the centers are set. The cookies will firm up as they cool.
8. **Cool:**
    - Allow the cookies to cool on the baking sheet for a few minutes before transferring them to a wire rack to cool completely.
9. **Prepare Glaze (Optional):**
    - If using the glaze, whisk together the powdered sugar and sake until smooth. Drizzle over the cooled cookies. For added flavor, you can mix in some lemon or orange zest.

Tips:

- **Sake:** Use a smooth, slightly sweet sake for the best results. The sake's subtle flavors will infuse into the cookies, adding a unique and pleasant taste.
- **Texture:** These cookies will have a soft, tender crumb with a delicate hint of sake flavor. If the dough is too soft to handle, chill it in the refrigerator for about 30 minutes before baking.
- **Flavor Variations:** For an added twist, consider incorporating a bit of citrus zest (like lemon or orange) into the dough or glaze for a refreshing contrast to the sake's flavor.
- **Storage:** Store the cookies in an airtight container at room temperature for up to a week. They can also be frozen for longer storage.

These sake-infused cookies offer a delightful blend of traditional cookie sweetness with a sophisticated hint of sake, making them a special treat for any occasion. Enjoy the unique flavor profile!

Japanese Spiced Butter Cookies

Ingredients:

- **1 cup (2 sticks, 230g) unsalted butter, softened**
- **1 cup (200g) granulated sugar**
- **1/2 cup (100g) packed brown sugar**
- **1 large egg**
- **1 teaspoon vanilla extract**
- **2 1/4 cups (285g) all-purpose flour**
- **1/2 teaspoon baking powder**
- **1/4 teaspoon baking soda**
- **1/4 teaspoon salt**

Spice Mix:

- **1 teaspoon shichimi togarashi** (a Japanese spice blend that typically includes chili pepper, sesame seeds, and other spices; adjust to taste)
- **1 teaspoon yuzu zest** (optional, for a citrusy note; can substitute with lemon or orange zest)
- **1/2 teaspoon ground ginger** (optional, for warmth)

Optional Glaze:

- **1/2 cup (60g) powdered sugar**
- **1-2 tablespoons yuzu juice** (or lemon juice as a substitute)

Instructions:

1. **Preheat Oven:**
    - Preheat your oven to 350°F (175°C) and line a baking sheet with parchment paper.
2. **Cream Butter and Sugars:**
    - In a large bowl, cream together the softened butter, granulated sugar, and brown sugar until light and fluffy.
3. **Add Egg and Vanilla:**
    - Beat in the egg and vanilla extract until well combined.
4. **Mix Dry Ingredients:**
    - In a separate bowl, whisk together the flour, baking powder, baking soda, salt, and the spice mix (shichimi togarashi, yuzu zest, and ground ginger).
5. **Combine Ingredients:**
    - Gradually add the dry ingredients to the wet mixture, mixing until just combined.
6. **Shape Cookies:**

- Scoop tablespoon-sized portions of dough and place them on the prepared baking sheet, spacing them about 2 inches apart. Flatten each ball slightly with the back of a spoon or your fingers.
7. **Bake:**
    - Bake in the preheated oven for 10-12 minutes, or until the edges are lightly golden and the centers are set.
8. **Cool:**
    - Allow the cookies to cool on the baking sheet for a few minutes before transferring them to a wire rack to cool completely.
9. **Prepare Glaze (Optional):**
    - If using the glaze, whisk together the powdered sugar and yuzu juice (or lemon juice) until smooth. Drizzle over the cooled cookies for a touch of citrus sweetness.

Tips:

- **Shichimi Togarashi:** This spice blend adds a unique depth to the cookies. Adjust the amount based on your heat tolerance and flavor preference.
- **Yuzu Zest:** Adds a bright, citrusy flavor. If you can't find yuzu, lemon or orange zest can be used as a substitute.
- **Texture:** The cookies should be tender with a slight crunch, and the spices will give them a unique flavor twist. If the dough is too soft to handle, chill it in the refrigerator for about 30 minutes before baking.
- **Flavor Variations:** Feel free to experiment with other spices like matcha powder or ground cinnamon to create different flavor profiles.
- **Storage:** Store the cookies in an airtight container at room temperature for up to a week. They can also be frozen for longer storage.

These Japanese spiced butter cookies offer a delightful fusion of traditional cookie sweetness and intriguing Japanese spices, making them a perfect treat for any time of year. Enjoy!

Sweet Soy Glazed Cookies

Ingredients:

For the Cookies:

- 1 cup (2 sticks, 230g) unsalted butter, softened
- 1 cup (200g) granulated sugar
- 1/2 cup (100g) packed brown sugar
- 1 large egg
- 1 teaspoon vanilla extract
- 2 1/4 cups (285g) all-purpose flour
- 1/2 teaspoon baking powder
- 1/4 teaspoon baking soda
- 1/4 teaspoon salt

For the Sweet Soy Glaze:

- 1/4 cup (60ml) soy sauce
- 1/2 cup (100g) granulated sugar
- 1 tablespoon cornstarch
- 1 tablespoon water

Instructions:

1. **Preheat Oven:**
   - Preheat your oven to 350°F (175°C) and line a baking sheet with parchment paper.
2. **Cream Butter and Sugars:**
   - In a large bowl, cream together the softened butter, granulated sugar, and brown sugar until light and fluffy.
3. **Add Egg and Vanilla:**
   - Beat in the egg and vanilla extract until well combined.
4. **Mix Dry Ingredients:**
   - In a separate bowl, whisk together the flour, baking powder, baking soda, and salt.
5. **Combine Ingredients:**
   - Gradually add the dry ingredients to the wet mixture, mixing until just combined.
6. **Shape Cookies:**
   - Scoop tablespoon-sized portions of dough and place them on the prepared baking sheet, spacing them about 2 inches apart. Flatten each ball slightly with the back of a spoon or your fingers.
7. **Bake:**

- Bake in the preheated oven for 10-12 minutes, or until the edges are lightly golden and the centers are set.
8. **Cool:**
    - Allow the cookies to cool on the baking sheet for a few minutes before transferring them to a wire rack to cool completely.
9. **Prepare Sweet Soy Glaze:**
    - In a small saucepan, combine the soy sauce and granulated sugar. Heat over medium heat, stirring until the sugar is fully dissolved.
    - In a small bowl, mix the cornstarch and water to create a slurry. Gradually add this slurry to the saucepan, stirring constantly.
    - Continue to cook the glaze until it thickens slightly, about 1-2 minutes. Remove from heat and let it cool slightly.
10. **Glaze Cookies:**
    - Once the cookies have cooled, brush or drizzle the sweet soy glaze over the top of each cookie. Let the glaze set before serving.

Tips:

- **Soy Sauce:** Use a mild soy sauce or light soy sauce to avoid overwhelming the cookies with a salty flavor.
- **Glaze Consistency:** The glaze should be thick enough to coat the cookies but still pourable. If it becomes too thick, you can thin it with a little water.
- **Texture:** The cookies will have a tender crumb, and the glaze will add a glossy finish with a hint of umami. If the dough is too soft to handle, chill it in the refrigerator for about 30 minutes before baking.
- **Storage:** Store the cookies in an airtight container at room temperature for up to a week. The glaze will remain sticky, so store them in a single layer to prevent sticking.

These sweet soy glazed cookies offer a unique fusion of flavors, combining the sweetness of traditional cookies with a savory soy glaze for a memorable treat. Enjoy!

Japanese Plum Cookies

Ingredients:

For the Cookies:

- 1 cup (2 sticks, 230g) unsalted butter, softened
- 1 cup (200g) granulated sugar
- 1/2 cup (100g) packed brown sugar
- 1 large egg
- 1 teaspoon vanilla extract
- 2 cups (250g) all-purpose flour
- 1/2 teaspoon baking powder
- 1/4 teaspoon baking soda
- 1/4 teaspoon salt

For the Plum Filling:

- 1/2 cup (120g) Japanese plum jam or preserves (ume jam or umeboshi paste works well; if using umeboshi paste, adjust the quantity to taste as it can be quite tart)

Optional Glaze:

- 1/2 cup (60g) powdered sugar
- 1-2 tablespoons plum juice or water (for a light glaze)

Instructions:

1. **Preheat Oven:**
    - Preheat your oven to 350°F (175°C) and line a baking sheet with parchment paper.
2. **Prepare Plum Filling:**
    - If using umeboshi paste or plum preserves, make sure it's smooth. If it's chunky, you might want to blend it slightly to make it easier to work with.
3. **Cream Butter and Sugars:**
    - In a large bowl, cream together the softened butter, granulated sugar, and brown sugar until light and fluffy.
4. **Add Egg and Vanilla:**
    - Beat in the egg and vanilla extract until well combined.
5. **Mix Dry Ingredients:**
    - In a separate bowl, whisk together the flour, baking powder, baking soda, and salt.
6. **Combine Ingredients:**
    - Gradually add the dry ingredients to the wet mixture, mixing until just combined.

7. **Shape Cookies:**
   - Scoop tablespoon-sized portions of dough and flatten them slightly. Place a small teaspoon of plum filling in the center of half of the dough portions. Top with the remaining dough portions and seal the edges by pinching the dough together. Flatten each filled dough ball slightly to form cookies.
8. **Bake:**
   - Bake in the preheated oven for 12-15 minutes, or until the edges are lightly golden and the centers are set.
9. **Cool:**
   - Allow the cookies to cool on the baking sheet for a few minutes before transferring them to a wire rack to cool completely.
10. **Prepare Glaze (Optional):**
    - If using the glaze, whisk together the powdered sugar and plum juice (or water) until smooth. Drizzle over the cooled cookies for an extra touch of sweetness.

Tips:

- **Plum Filling:** Adjust the amount of plum filling based on your taste preference. If the filling is too tart, you can sweeten it slightly or adjust the amount used.
- **Dough Handling:** If the dough is too soft to handle, chill it in the refrigerator for about 30 minutes before shaping.
- **Texture:** The cookies will have a tender, buttery texture with a sweet and tangy plum center. Ensure that the edges are well sealed to prevent the filling from leaking out during baking.
- **Storage:** Store the cookies in an airtight container at room temperature for up to a week. They can also be frozen for longer storage.

These Japanese plum cookies bring together the classic flavors of Japanese plums with a comforting cookie base, offering a unique and delicious treat that's perfect for any occasion. Enjoy!

Black Sugar Cookies

Ingredients:

- **1 cup (2 sticks, 230g) unsalted butter, softened**
- **1 cup (200g) black sugar** (kokuto or dark brown sugar can be used as a substitute)
- **1/2 cup (100g) granulated sugar**
- **1 large egg**
- **1 teaspoon vanilla extract**
- **2 1/4 cups (285g) all-purpose flour**
- **1/2 teaspoon baking powder**
- **1/4 teaspoon baking soda**
- **1/4 teaspoon salt**

Optional Glaze:

- **1/2 cup (60g) powdered sugar**
- **1-2 tablespoons milk or water**

Instructions:

1. **Preheat Oven:**
   - Preheat your oven to 350°F (175°C) and line a baking sheet with parchment paper.
2. **Cream Butter and Sugars:**
   - In a large bowl, cream together the softened butter, black sugar, and granulated sugar until light and fluffy.
3. **Add Egg and Vanilla:**
   - Beat in the egg and vanilla extract until well combined.
4. **Mix Dry Ingredients:**
   - In a separate bowl, whisk together the flour, baking powder, baking soda, and salt.
5. **Combine Ingredients:**
   - Gradually add the dry ingredients to the wet mixture, mixing until just combined.
6. **Shape Cookies:**
   - Scoop tablespoon-sized portions of dough and place them on the prepared baking sheet, spacing them about 2 inches apart. Flatten each ball slightly with the back of a spoon or your fingers.
7. **Bake:**
   - Bake in the preheated oven for 10-12 minutes, or until the edges are lightly golden and the centers are set.
8. **Cool:**

- Allow the cookies to cool on the baking sheet for a few minutes before transferring them to a wire rack to cool completely.
9. **Prepare Glaze (Optional):**
    - If using the glaze, whisk together the powdered sugar and milk or water until smooth. Drizzle over the cooled cookies for a touch of sweetness.

Tips:

- **Black Sugar:** Black sugar (kokuto) can be found in Asian markets or online. If you can't find black sugar, dark brown sugar is a good substitute, though the flavor will be slightly different.
- **Texture:** The cookies should have a soft, tender crumb with a rich, caramelized flavor. If the dough is too soft to handle, chill it in the refrigerator for about 30 minutes before baking.
- **Flavor Variations:** You can enhance the flavor by adding spices like ground cinnamon or ginger, or a touch of sea salt on top before baking for a sweet-savory contrast.
- **Storage:** Store the cookies in an airtight container at room temperature for up to a week. They can also be frozen for longer storage.

These black sugar cookies offer a unique twist on the classic cookie, with the rich and deep flavor of black sugar making them a special treat. Enjoy the distinctive taste!

Yuzu and Ginger Cookies

Ingredients:

For the Cookies:

- **1 cup (2 sticks, 230g) unsalted butter, softened**
- **1 cup (200g) granulated sugar**
- **1/2 cup (100g) brown sugar, packed**
- **1 large egg**
- **1 tablespoon yuzu zest** (or lemon zest as a substitute if yuzu is unavailable)
- **1 tablespoon yuzu juice** (or lemon juice as a substitute)
- **1 teaspoon vanilla extract**
- **2 1/4 cups (285g) all-purpose flour**
- **1 teaspoon ground ginger**
- **1/2 teaspoon baking powder**
- **1/4 teaspoon baking soda**
- **1/4 teaspoon salt**

Optional Glaze:

- **1/2 cup (60g) powdered sugar**
- **1-2 tablespoons yuzu juice** (or lemon juice)

Instructions:

1. **Preheat Oven:**
   - Preheat your oven to 350°F (175°C) and line a baking sheet with parchment paper.
2. **Cream Butter and Sugars:**
   - In a large bowl, cream together the softened butter, granulated sugar, and brown sugar until light and fluffy.
3. **Add Egg, Yuzu, and Vanilla:**
   - Beat in the egg until well combined. Mix in the yuzu zest, yuzu juice, and vanilla extract.
4. **Mix Dry Ingredients:**
   - In a separate bowl, whisk together the flour, ground ginger, baking powder, baking soda, and salt.
5. **Combine Ingredients:**
   - Gradually add the dry ingredients to the wet mixture, mixing until just combined. The dough will be slightly soft.
6. **Shape Cookies:**

- Scoop tablespoon-sized portions of dough and place them on the prepared baking sheet, spacing them about 2 inches apart. Flatten each ball slightly with the back of a spoon or your fingers.

7. **Bake:**
   - Bake in the preheated oven for 10-12 minutes, or until the edges are lightly golden and the centers are set. The cookies will firm up as they cool.
8. **Cool:**
   - Allow the cookies to cool on the baking sheet for a few minutes before transferring them to a wire rack to cool completely.
9. **Prepare Glaze (Optional):**
   - If using the glaze, whisk together the powdered sugar and yuzu juice (or lemon juice) until smooth. Drizzle over the cooled cookies for a touch of citrus sweetness.

Tips:

- **Yuzu Juice and Zest:** Yuzu has a unique flavor that's a blend of lemon, lime, and grapefruit. If you can't find fresh yuzu, yuzu juice and zest can be found in Asian markets or online. Lemon or lime zest and juice can be used as substitutes.
- **Ginger:** Freshly grated ginger can be used for a more intense flavor, but ground ginger works well for a more subtle spice.
- **Texture:** The cookies should have a tender, slightly chewy texture with a zesty citrus flavor and a hint of spice. If the dough is too soft, chill it in the refrigerator for about 30 minutes before baking.
- **Flavor Variations:** You can add a pinch of ground cinnamon or cloves for additional warmth, or top the cookies with a sprinkle of sugar before baking for a touch of sparkle.
- **Storage:** Store the cookies in an airtight container at room temperature for up to a week. They can also be frozen for longer storage.

These yuzu and ginger cookies are a delightful blend of citrus and spice, perfect for any occasion. Enjoy the refreshing and comforting flavors!

Tamarind and Coconut Cookies

Ingredients:

For the Cookies:

- **1 cup (2 sticks, 230g) unsalted butter, softened**
- **1 cup (200g) granulated sugar**
- **1/2 cup (100g) packed brown sugar**
- **1 large egg**
- **1 teaspoon vanilla extract**
- **1/4 cup (60g) tamarind paste** (adjust according to taste; tamarind concentrate can also be used)
- **2 cups (250g) all-purpose flour**
- **1/2 teaspoon baking powder**
- **1/4 teaspoon baking soda**
- **1/4 teaspoon salt**
- **1 cup (90g) shredded coconut** (sweetened or unsweetened based on preference)

Optional Glaze:

- **1/2 cup (60g) powdered sugar**
- **1-2 tablespoons tamarind juice** (or water, for thinning the glaze)

Instructions:

1. **Preheat Oven:**
    - Preheat your oven to 350°F (175°C) and line a baking sheet with parchment paper.
2. **Cream Butter and Sugars:**
    - In a large bowl, cream together the softened butter, granulated sugar, and brown sugar until light and fluffy.
3. **Add Egg, Vanilla, and Tamarind:**
    - Beat in the egg and vanilla extract until well combined. Mix in the tamarind paste until fully incorporated. The mixture may look slightly curdled; that's okay.
4. **Mix Dry Ingredients:**
    - In a separate bowl, whisk together the flour, baking powder, baking soda, and salt.
5. **Combine Ingredients:**
    - Gradually add the dry ingredients to the wet mixture, mixing until just combined. Stir in the shredded coconut.
6. **Shape Cookies:**

- Scoop tablespoon-sized portions of dough and place them on the prepared baking sheet, spacing them about 2 inches apart. Flatten each ball slightly with the back of a spoon or your fingers.

7. **Bake:**
    - Bake in the preheated oven for 10-12 minutes, or until the edges are lightly golden and the centers are set.
8. **Cool:**
    - Allow the cookies to cool on the baking sheet for a few minutes before transferring them to a wire rack to cool completely.
9. **Prepare Glaze (Optional):**
    - If using the glaze, whisk together the powdered sugar and tamarind juice (or water) until smooth. Drizzle over the cooled cookies for a touch of extra sweetness and tanginess.

Tips:

- **Tamarind Paste:** Adjust the amount based on how strong you want the tamarind flavor to be. Tamarind paste is quite tangy and sweet, so a little goes a long way.
- **Coconut:** If you prefer a less sweet cookie, use unsweetened shredded coconut. Sweetened coconut adds extra sweetness.
- **Texture:** The cookies will have a chewy texture with a rich coconut flavor and a hint of tanginess from the tamarind. If the dough is too soft to handle, chill it in the refrigerator for about 30 minutes before baking.
- **Flavor Variations:** You can add a pinch of ground cinnamon or cardamom for additional warmth and depth of flavor.
- **Storage:** Store the cookies in an airtight container at room temperature for up to a week. They can also be frozen for longer storage.

These tamarind and coconut cookies offer a delightful blend of flavors that's both exotic and comforting, making them a special treat for any occasion. Enjoy!

Japanese Pumpkin Pie Cookies

Ingredients:

For the Cookies:

- 1 cup (2 sticks, 230g) unsalted butter, softened
- 1 cup (200g) granulated sugar
- 1/2 cup (100g) packed brown sugar
- 1 large egg
- 1 teaspoon vanilla extract
- 1 cup (240g) pumpkin puree (preferably kabocha puree or canned pumpkin)
- 2 1/4 cups (285g) all-purpose flour
- 1/2 teaspoon baking powder
- 1/4 teaspoon baking soda
- 1/4 teaspoon salt
- 1 teaspoon ground cinnamon
- 1/2 teaspoon ground ginger
- 1/4 teaspoon ground nutmeg
- 1/4 teaspoon ground cloves

For the Pumpkin Pie Spice Sugar Coating (Optional):

- 1/4 cup (50g) granulated sugar
- 1 teaspoon ground cinnamon
- 1/2 teaspoon ground ginger

Instructions:

1. **Preheat Oven:**
   - Preheat your oven to 350°F (175°C) and line a baking sheet with parchment paper.
2. **Cream Butter and Sugars:**
   - In a large bowl, cream together the softened butter, granulated sugar, and brown sugar until light and fluffy.
3. **Add Egg, Vanilla, and Pumpkin:**
   - Beat in the egg and vanilla extract until well combined. Mix in the pumpkin puree until fully incorporated.
4. **Mix Dry Ingredients:**
   - In a separate bowl, whisk together the flour, baking powder, baking soda, salt, cinnamon, ginger, nutmeg, and cloves.
5. **Combine Ingredients:**
   - Gradually add the dry ingredients to the wet mixture, mixing until just combined.

6. **Shape Cookies:**
   - Scoop tablespoon-sized portions of dough and place them on the prepared baking sheet, spacing them about 2 inches apart. Flatten each ball slightly with the back of a spoon or your fingers.
7. **Prepare Sugar Coating (Optional):**
   - In a small bowl, mix together the granulated sugar, ground cinnamon, and ground ginger. Sprinkle or roll each cookie in the sugar mixture before baking for added flavor and a slightly crunchy exterior.
8. **Bake:**
   - Bake in the preheated oven for 12-15 minutes, or until the edges are lightly golden and the centers are set.
9. **Cool:**
   - Allow the cookies to cool on the baking sheet for a few minutes before transferring them to a wire rack to cool completely.

Tips:

- **Pumpkin Puree:** Use pumpkin puree that is smooth and not too watery. If using kabocha, roast and puree it until smooth. Ensure there's no excess moisture in the puree.
- **Spices:** Adjust the spices to your taste preference. Adding a bit more or less of each spice can change the flavor profile.
- **Texture:** The cookies should be soft and slightly cakey, with a warm, spiced flavor. If the dough is too soft to handle, chill it in the refrigerator for about 30 minutes before baking.
- **Storage:** Store the cookies in an airtight container at room temperature for up to a week. They can also be frozen for longer storage.

These Japanese pumpkin pie cookies offer a delightful twist on classic pumpkin pie flavors, combining them into a convenient and delicious cookie format. Enjoy the warm and comforting taste!

Matcha and Red Bean Cookies

Ingredients:

For the Cookies:

- 1 cup (2 sticks, 230g) unsalted butter, softened
- 1 cup (200g) granulated sugar
- 1/2 cup (100g) packed brown sugar
- 1 large egg
- 1 teaspoon vanilla extract
- 2 1/4 cups (285g) all-purpose flour
- 2 tablespoons matcha powder (adjust to taste for stronger or milder flavor)
- 1/2 teaspoon baking powder
- 1/4 teaspoon baking soda
- 1/4 teaspoon salt

For the Red Bean Filling:

- 1/2 cup (120g) sweet red bean paste (anko, preferably smooth; can be found in Asian markets or online)

Instructions:

1. **Preheat Oven:**
    - Preheat your oven to 350°F (175°C) and line a baking sheet with parchment paper.
2. **Cream Butter and Sugars:**
    - In a large bowl, cream together the softened butter, granulated sugar, and brown sugar until light and fluffy.
3. **Add Egg and Vanilla:**
    - Beat in the egg and vanilla extract until well combined.
4. **Mix Dry Ingredients:**
    - In a separate bowl, whisk together the flour, matcha powder, baking powder, baking soda, and salt.
5. **Combine Ingredients:**
    - Gradually add the dry ingredients to the wet mixture, mixing until just combined.
6. **Prepare Red Bean Filling:**
    - If the red bean paste is too thick, you can slightly warm it to make it easier to work with. Use a spoon to scoop small amounts of red bean paste (about 1 teaspoon each) and roll them into balls.
7. **Shape Cookies:**

- Scoop tablespoon-sized portions of cookie dough and flatten them slightly. Place a ball of red bean paste in the center of each flattened dough portion. Fold the edges of the dough around the red bean paste and roll the dough into a ball, sealing the filling inside. Place the cookies on the prepared baking sheet, spacing them about 2 inches apart.
8. **Bake:**
    - Bake in the preheated oven for 12-15 minutes, or until the edges are lightly golden and the centers are set.
9. **Cool:**
    - Allow the cookies to cool on the baking sheet for a few minutes before transferring them to a wire rack to cool completely.

Tips:

- **Matcha Powder:** Use high-quality matcha powder for the best flavor. Adjust the amount of matcha to suit your taste preference; more matcha will give a stronger green tea flavor.
- **Red Bean Paste:** Ensure that the red bean paste is smooth and not too runny. If it's too thick to work with, you can warm it slightly to make it easier to handle.
- **Texture:** The cookies will have a tender texture with a slightly chewy center where the red bean paste is hidden. If the dough is too soft, chill it in the refrigerator for about 30 minutes before shaping.
- **Flavor Variations:** For an extra touch, you can sprinkle a little bit of coarse sugar on top of the cookies before baking or add a touch of sea salt for contrast.
- **Storage:** Store the cookies in an airtight container at room temperature for up to a week. They can also be frozen for longer storage.

These matcha and red bean cookies offer a delightful combination of flavors and textures, making them a unique and enjoyable treat. Enjoy the perfect blend of green tea and sweet red bean in every bite!

Kinako and Black Sesame Cookies

Ingredients:

For the Cookies:

- 1 cup (2 sticks, 230g) unsalted butter, softened
- 1 cup (200g) granulated sugar
- 1/2 cup (100g) packed brown sugar
- 1 large egg
- 1 teaspoon vanilla extract
- 1 cup (100g) kinako (roasted soybean flour)
- 1 cup (100g) black sesame seeds (toasted if desired, for enhanced flavor)
- 1 3/4 cups (220g) all-purpose flour
- 1/2 teaspoon baking powder
- 1/4 teaspoon baking soda
- 1/4 teaspoon salt

Optional Topping:

- 1/4 cup (30g) black sesame seeds (for rolling the cookie dough balls)
- 1 tablespoon kinako (for dusting)

Instructions:

1. **Preheat Oven:**
    - Preheat your oven to 350°F (175°C) and line a baking sheet with parchment paper.
2. **Cream Butter and Sugars:**
    - In a large bowl, cream together the softened butter, granulated sugar, and brown sugar until light and fluffy.
3. **Add Egg and Vanilla:**
    - Beat in the egg and vanilla extract until well combined.
4. **Mix Dry Ingredients:**
    - In a separate bowl, whisk together the flour, kinako, black sesame seeds, baking powder, baking soda, and salt.
5. **Combine Ingredients:**
    - Gradually add the dry ingredients to the wet mixture, mixing until just combined.
6. **Shape Cookies:**
    - Scoop tablespoon-sized portions of dough and roll into balls. If using, roll the dough balls in black sesame seeds and/or kinako to coat them lightly. Place them on the prepared baking sheet, spacing them about 2 inches apart. Flatten each ball slightly with the back of a spoon or your fingers.

7. **Bake:**
   - Bake in the preheated oven for 10-12 minutes, or until the edges are lightly golden and the centers are set. The cookies will firm up as they cool.
8. **Cool:**
   - Allow the cookies to cool on the baking sheet for a few minutes before transferring them to a wire rack to cool completely.

Tips:

- **Kinako:** Kinako adds a nutty, roasted flavor to the cookies. It can be found in Asian markets or online. If kinako is unavailable, you can use finely ground toasted soybeans as a substitute.
- **Black Sesame Seeds:** Toasting the black sesame seeds can enhance their flavor. Simply toast them in a dry skillet over medium heat until they become fragrant and slightly darker.
- **Texture:** The cookies will have a slightly crumbly and tender texture with a delightful crunch from the black sesame seeds. If the dough is too soft, chill it in the refrigerator for about 30 minutes before baking.
- **Flavor Variations:** You can add a pinch of sea salt to the dough or sprinkle some on top of the cookies before baking for added flavor contrast.
- **Storage:** Store the cookies in an airtight container at room temperature for up to a week. They can also be frozen for longer storage.

These kinako and black sesame cookies offer a wonderful combination of flavors and textures, making them a unique and enjoyable treat. Enjoy the nutty and slightly sweet notes in every bite!

Sesame and Honey Cookies

Ingredients:

For the Cookies:

- 1 cup (2 sticks, 230g) unsalted butter, softened
- 1 cup (200g) granulated sugar
- 1/2 cup (120g) honey (preferably mild-flavored, like clover or acacia)
- 1 large egg
- 1 teaspoon vanilla extract
- 2 1/4 cups (285g) all-purpose flour
- 1/2 teaspoon baking powder
- 1/4 teaspoon baking soda
- 1/4 teaspoon salt
- 1/2 cup (70g) sesame seeds (toasted if desired for enhanced flavor)

Optional Topping:

- 1/4 cup (30g) sesame seeds (for rolling the cookie dough balls)

Instructions:

1. **Preheat Oven:**
   - Preheat your oven to 350°F (175°C) and line a baking sheet with parchment paper.
2. **Cream Butter and Sugar:**
   - In a large bowl, cream together the softened butter and granulated sugar until light and fluffy.
3. **Add Honey, Egg, and Vanilla:**
   - Beat in the honey until well combined. Add the egg and vanilla extract, mixing until fully incorporated.
4. **Mix Dry Ingredients:**
   - In a separate bowl, whisk together the flour, baking powder, baking soda, and salt.
5. **Combine Ingredients:**
   - Gradually add the dry ingredients to the wet mixture, mixing until just combined. Stir in the sesame seeds.
6. **Shape Cookies:**
   - Scoop tablespoon-sized portions of dough and roll them into balls. If using, roll the dough balls in sesame seeds to coat them lightly. Place them on the prepared baking sheet, spacing them about 2 inches apart. Flatten each ball slightly with the back of a spoon or your fingers.

7. **Bake:**
    - Bake in the preheated oven for 10-12 minutes, or until the edges are lightly golden and the centers are set. The cookies will firm up as they cool.
8. **Cool:**
    - Allow the cookies to cool on the baking sheet for a few minutes before transferring them to a wire rack to cool completely.

Tips:

- **Sesame Seeds:** Toasting the sesame seeds before adding them to the dough can enhance their flavor. To toast, place them in a dry skillet over medium heat and stir frequently until fragrant and lightly browned.
- **Honey:** Use a mild-flavored honey so it doesn't overpower the sesame. If your honey is very thick, you can warm it slightly to make it easier to mix.
- **Texture:** The cookies will have a tender, slightly chewy texture with a delightful crunch from the sesame seeds. If the dough is too soft to handle, chill it in the refrigerator for about 30 minutes before baking.
- **Flavor Variations:** For an extra touch, you can sprinkle a little sea salt on top of the cookies before baking or add a pinch of ground cinnamon or ginger to the dough for additional warmth.
- **Storage:** Store the cookies in an airtight container at room temperature for up to a week. They can also be frozen for longer storage.

These sesame and honey cookies are a perfect blend of nutty and sweet flavors, making them a delightful treat for any occasion. Enjoy the crispy and chewy goodness!

Sweet Potato and Cinnamon Cookies

Ingredients:

For the Cookies:

- 1 cup (2 sticks, 230g) unsalted butter, softened
- 1 cup (200g) granulated sugar
- 1/2 cup (100g) brown sugar, packed
- 1 large egg
- 1 cup (200g) mashed sweet potato (cooked and cooled; can use canned sweet potato puree if preferred)
- 1 teaspoon vanilla extract
- 2 1/4 cups (285g) all-purpose flour
- 1 teaspoon ground cinnamon
- 1/2 teaspoon ground nutmeg
- 1/2 teaspoon baking powder
- 1/4 teaspoon baking soda
- 1/4 teaspoon salt

Optional Topping:

- 1 tablespoon granulated sugar
- 1/2 teaspoon ground cinnamon

Instructions:

1. **Prepare Sweet Potato:**
   - If using fresh sweet potato, peel, chop, and boil or bake until tender. Mash until smooth and let it cool completely before using. Alternatively, you can use canned sweet potato puree.
2. **Preheat Oven:**
   - Preheat your oven to 350°F (175°C) and line a baking sheet with parchment paper.
3. **Cream Butter and Sugars:**
   - In a large bowl, cream together the softened butter, granulated sugar, and brown sugar until light and fluffy.
4. **Add Egg, Sweet Potato, and Vanilla:**
   - Beat in the egg, mashed sweet potato, and vanilla extract until well combined.
5. **Mix Dry Ingredients:**
   - In a separate bowl, whisk together the flour, ground cinnamon, ground nutmeg, baking powder, baking soda, and salt.
6. **Combine Ingredients:**

- Gradually add the dry ingredients to the wet mixture, mixing until just combined.
7. **Shape Cookies:**
    - Scoop tablespoon-sized portions of dough and place them on the prepared baking sheet, spacing them about 2 inches apart. Flatten each ball slightly with the back of a spoon or your fingers.
8. **Optional Topping:**
    - If desired, mix the granulated sugar and ground cinnamon together in a small bowl and sprinkle a little on top of each cookie before baking for extra flavor and a touch of sweetness.
9. **Bake:**
    - Bake in the preheated oven for 12-15 minutes, or until the edges are lightly golden and the centers are set.
10. **Cool:**
    - Allow the cookies to cool on the baking sheet for a few minutes before transferring them to a wire rack to cool completely.

Tips:

- **Sweet Potato:** Ensure that the sweet potato is well-mashed and not too wet. Excess moisture can affect the texture of the cookies.
- **Spices:** Adjust the amount of cinnamon and nutmeg to your taste. You can also add a pinch of ground ginger for extra warmth.
- **Texture:** The cookies should be soft and slightly chewy with a subtle sweetness from the sweet potato. If the dough is too soft to handle, chill it in the refrigerator for about 30 minutes before baking.
- **Storage:** Store the cookies in an airtight container at room temperature for up to a week. They can also be frozen for longer storage.

These sweet potato and cinnamon cookies offer a delightful blend of flavors and textures, making them a perfect treat for any time of year. Enjoy the comforting taste of sweet potatoes and cinnamon in every bite!

Cherry Blossom Macarons

Ingredients:

For the Macaron Shells:

- **1 cup (100g) almond flour**
- **1 3/4 cups (200g) powdered sugar**
- **3 large egg whites** (at room temperature)
- **1/4 teaspoon cream of tartar**
- **1/2 cup (100g) granulated sugar**
- **1 tablespoon cherry blossom powder** (sakura powder; can be found in Asian markets or online; or use a few drops of cherry blossom extract as a substitute)
- **Pink gel food coloring** (optional, for a pastel pink color)

For the Cherry Blossom Buttercream Filling:

- **1/2 cup (1 stick, 115g) unsalted butter, softened**
- **1 1/2 cups (190g) powdered sugar**
- **1 tablespoon cherry blossom powder** (or a few drops of cherry blossom extract)
- **1-2 tablespoons heavy cream** (or milk, to reach desired consistency)
- **1/2 teaspoon vanilla extract**

Instructions:

1. **Prepare Baking Sheets:**
   - Line two baking sheets with parchment paper or silicone baking mats. If using parchment paper, you can draw circles on the underside of the paper to help guide the size of your macarons.
2. **Sift Dry Ingredients:**
   - Sift the almond flour and powdered sugar together into a bowl to remove any lumps. Set aside.
3. **Whip Egg Whites:**
   - In a clean, dry mixing bowl, beat the egg whites with an electric mixer on medium speed until they become frothy. Add the cream of tartar and continue to beat until soft peaks form.
4. **Add Granulated Sugar:**
   - Gradually add the granulated sugar, a tablespoon at a time, while continuing to beat the egg whites. Increase the mixer speed to high and beat until stiff, glossy peaks form.
5. **Add Cherry Blossom Powder and Color:**
   - Gently fold in the cherry blossom powder (or extract) and pink gel food coloring (if using) into the meringue until well combined. Be careful not to overmix.

6. **Incorporate Dry Ingredients:**
   - Gently fold the sifted almond flour and powdered sugar mixture into the meringue in two additions. Use a spatula to fold the mixture, making sure to incorporate all the dry ingredients. The batter should flow slowly off the spatula and form a ribbon-like texture.
7. **Pipe Macarons:**
   - Transfer the macaron batter to a piping bag fitted with a round tip. Pipe small circles (about 1.5 inches in diameter) onto the prepared baking sheets, spacing them about 1 inch apart. Tap the baking sheets firmly on the counter to release any air bubbles and smooth the tops.
8. **Rest the Macarons:**
   - Let the piped macarons sit at room temperature for about 30-60 minutes, or until they form a skin that is dry to the touch. This step is crucial for developing the characteristic macaron "feet."
9. **Preheat Oven:**
   - Preheat your oven to 300°F (150°C).
10. **Bake:**
    - Bake the macarons in the preheated oven for 15-18 minutes, or until the shells are set and can be easily lifted from the baking sheet. If using multiple racks, rotate the baking sheets halfway through baking for even results.
11. **Cool:**
    - Allow the macarons to cool completely on the baking sheets before removing them.
12. **Prepare Filling:**
    - In a mixing bowl, beat the softened butter until creamy. Gradually add the powdered sugar and beat until smooth. Mix in the cherry blossom powder (or extract), vanilla extract, and enough heavy cream to reach your desired consistency.
13. **Assemble Macarons:**
    - Pair up the macaron shells of similar sizes. Pipe or spread the cherry blossom buttercream filling onto the flat side of one shell, then gently press the other shell on top to create a sandwich.
14. **Mature:**
    - For the best flavor and texture, let the assembled macarons sit in the refrigerator for 24 hours before serving. This allows the flavors to meld and the filling to soften the shells.

Tips:

- **Cherry Blossom Powder:** If you can't find cherry blossom powder, you can use cherry blossom extract, but adjust the amount to taste.
- **Macaronage:** Be careful not to overmix the batter. It should flow slowly off the spatula and form a ribbon when lifted.

- **Cooling:** Make sure the macarons are completely cooled before filling, or the filling may soften the shells.

These Cherry Blossom Macarons are a stunning and delicate treat that perfectly captures the essence of cherry blossoms. Enjoy the floral, sweet flavor in every bite!

Matcha Swirl Cookies

Ingredients:

For the Cookie Dough:

- 1 cup (2 sticks, 230g) unsalted butter, softened
- 1 cup (200g) granulated sugar
- 1/2 cup (100g) packed brown sugar
- 1 large egg
- 1 teaspoon vanilla extract
- 2 1/4 cups (285g) all-purpose flour
- 1/2 teaspoon baking powder
- 1/4 teaspoon baking soda
- 1/4 teaspoon salt

For the Matcha Dough:

- **2 tablespoons matcha powder** (high-quality for best flavor)
- **2 tablespoons granulated sugar** (optional, to sweeten the matcha portion)

Instructions:

1. **Prepare Baking Sheets:**
   - Preheat your oven to 350°F (175°C) and line two baking sheets with parchment paper.
2. **Make the Cookie Dough:**
   - In a large bowl, cream together the softened butter, granulated sugar, and brown sugar until light and fluffy.
   - Beat in the egg and vanilla extract until well combined.
3. **Mix Dry Ingredients:**
   - In a separate bowl, whisk together the flour, baking powder, baking soda, and salt.
4. **Combine Ingredients:**
   - Gradually add the dry ingredients to the wet mixture, mixing until just combined.
5. **Divide and Add Matcha:**
   - Divide the dough in half. In one half of the dough, sift in the matcha powder and mix until fully incorporated. If using, add 2 tablespoons of granulated sugar to the matcha dough to sweeten it slightly.
6. **Swirl the Dough:**
   - Roll out each portion of dough into rectangles on lightly floured surfaces. The matcha dough might be a little crumbly, so gently press it together as you roll.

- Place one rectangle of plain dough on top of the matcha dough rectangle, aligning the edges. Roll the stacked dough rectangles tightly into a log, similar to a jelly roll. If the dough is too soft, refrigerate it for about 30 minutes to make it easier to handle.

7. **Slice and Bake:**
    - Slice the dough log into approximately 1/4-inch thick rounds and place them on the prepared baking sheets, spacing them about 1 inch apart.
    - Bake in the preheated oven for 10-12 minutes, or until the edges are lightly golden and the centers are set.
8. **Cool:**
    - Allow the cookies to cool on the baking sheets for a few minutes before transferring them to a wire rack to cool completely.

Tips:

- **Matcha Powder:** Use high-quality matcha powder for the best flavor and vibrant color. Lower-quality matcha may have a more bitter taste.
- **Handling Dough:** If the dough is too soft, refrigerate it for about 30 minutes to make it easier to roll and slice.
- **Swirling:** For a more pronounced swirl effect, gently swirl the dough with a knife or skewer before baking, if desired.

These Matcha Swirl Cookies are a visually appealing and flavorful treat that pairs beautifully with tea or as a sweet snack. Enjoy the delicate balance of flavors and the lovely swirl pattern in every bite!

Mochi Rice Flour Cookies

Ingredients:

For the Cookies:

- 1 cup (200g) mochiko (glutinous rice flour)
- 1/2 cup (100g) granulated sugar
- 1/2 teaspoon baking powder
- 1/4 teaspoon salt
- 1/2 cup (1 stick, 115g) unsalted butter, softened
- 1 large egg
- 1 teaspoon vanilla extract

For Optional Toppings:

- **Powdered sugar** (for dusting)
- **Sesame seeds, or coconut flakes** (for added texture and flavor)

Instructions:

1. **Preheat Oven:**
   - Preheat your oven to 350°F (175°C) and line a baking sheet with parchment paper.
2. **Mix Dry Ingredients:**
   - In a medium bowl, whisk together the mochiko, granulated sugar, baking powder, and salt.
3. **Cream Butter and Sugar:**
   - In a large bowl, cream together the softened butter and granulated sugar until light and fluffy.
4. **Add Egg and Vanilla:**
   - Beat in the egg and vanilla extract until well combined.
5. **Combine Dry Ingredients:**
   - Gradually add the dry ingredients to the wet mixture, mixing until just combined. The dough will be slightly sticky.
6. **Shape Cookies:**
   - Scoop tablespoon-sized portions of dough and roll them into balls. Place them on the prepared baking sheet, spacing them about 1 inch apart. If desired, you can gently flatten the balls with the back of a spoon or your fingers. For added texture and flavor, roll the dough balls in sesame seeds or coconut flakes before placing them on the baking sheet.
7. **Bake:**

- Bake in the preheated oven for 10-12 minutes, or until the edges are lightly golden. The centers may appear slightly soft, but they will firm up as they cool.

8. **Cool:**
    - Allow the cookies to cool on the baking sheet for a few minutes before transferring them to a wire rack to cool completely.

9. **Optional Dusting:**
    - Once cooled, you can dust the cookies with powdered sugar for a touch of sweetness and a decorative finish.

Tips:

- **Mochiko:** Mochiko is a type of glutinous rice flour and is different from regular rice flour. It provides the chewy texture characteristic of mochi. It can be found in Asian markets or online.
- **Texture:** The cookies will have a chewy texture, similar to mochi, with a slightly crisp edge. If you prefer a firmer texture, you can bake them a bit longer, but be careful not to overbake.
- **Flavor Variations:** You can add mix-ins like chocolate chips, dried fruit, or nuts to the dough if desired. For a hint of flavor, consider adding a bit of matcha powder or cocoa powder.
- **Storage:** Store the cookies in an airtight container at room temperature for up to a week. They can also be frozen for longer storage.

These mochi rice flour cookies are a delightful treat with a unique texture and a subtle sweetness. They're perfect for enjoying with tea or as a special dessert!

Japanese Green Tea Shortbread

Ingredients:

For the Shortbread:

- **1 cup (2 sticks, 230g) unsalted butter, softened**
- **1/2 cup (100g) granulated sugar**
- **1/4 cup (50g) powdered sugar**
- **2 cups (250g) all-purpose flour**
- **2 tablespoons matcha powder** (high-quality for best flavor)
- **1/4 teaspoon salt**

For Optional Topping:

- **Powdered sugar** (for dusting)
- **Additional matcha powder** (for dusting)

Instructions:

1. **Preheat Oven:**
    - Preheat your oven to 325°F (160°C) and line a baking sheet with parchment paper.
2. **Cream Butter and Sugars:**
    - In a large bowl, cream together the softened butter, granulated sugar, and powdered sugar until light and fluffy.
3. **Add Dry Ingredients:**
    - In a separate bowl, whisk together the flour, matcha powder, and salt. Gradually add this mixture to the butter mixture, mixing until just combined. The dough will be crumbly.
4. **Shape the Dough:**
    - Turn the dough out onto a lightly floured surface and knead it gently until it comes together. Roll the dough out to about 1/4-inch thickness.
5. **Cut Out Cookies:**
    - Use cookie cutters to cut out shapes from the dough or simply cut the dough into squares or rectangles using a knife or a pizza cutter. Place the cookies on the prepared baking sheet, spacing them about 1 inch apart.
6. **Chill the Dough:**
    - For cleaner edges and to prevent spreading, chill the cut-out cookies in the refrigerator for about 15-20 minutes before baking.
7. **Bake:**
    - Bake in the preheated oven for 12-15 minutes, or until the edges are lightly golden. The centers should be pale.

8. **Cool:**
    - Allow the cookies to cool on the baking sheet for a few minutes before transferring them to a wire rack to cool completely.
9. **Optional Topping:**
    - Once cooled, you can dust the cookies with powdered sugar or a little additional matcha powder for a decorative finish.

Tips:

- **Matcha Powder:** Use high-quality matcha powder for the best flavor and color. Lower-quality matcha may have a more bitter taste.
- **Texture:** These shortbread cookies should be crisp and buttery with a delicate matcha flavor. The dough can be crumbly, but it should come together when gently kneaded.
- **Chilling the Dough:** Chilling helps to firm up the dough, making it easier to cut and ensuring the cookies hold their shape while baking.
- **Storage:** Store the cookies in an airtight container at room temperature for up to a week. They can also be frozen for longer storage.

Japanese Green Tea Shortbread offers a delightful blend of traditional buttery shortbread with the unique, sophisticated flavor of matcha. Enjoy them with a cup of tea or as a special treat!

Red Bean Mochi Cookies

Ingredients:

For the Cookies:

- 1 cup (2 sticks, 230g) unsalted butter, softened
- 1 cup (200g) granulated sugar
- 1/2 cup (100g) packed brown sugar
- 1 large egg
- 1 teaspoon vanilla extract
- 2 cups (250g) all-purpose flour
- 1/2 teaspoon baking powder
- 1/4 teaspoon baking soda
- 1/4 teaspoon salt
- 1 cup (240g) **sweet red bean paste** (anko; can use smooth or chunky)

For Optional Topping:

- **Powdered sugar** (for dusting)
- **Sesame seeds** or **shredded coconut** (for added texture)

Instructions:

1. **Prepare Baking Sheets:**
   - Preheat your oven to 350°F (175°C) and line two baking sheets with parchment paper.
2. **Mix Dry Ingredients:**
   - In a medium bowl, whisk together the flour, baking powder, baking soda, and salt. Set aside.
3. **Cream Butter and Sugars:**
   - In a large bowl, cream together the softened butter, granulated sugar, and brown sugar until light and fluffy.
4. **Add Egg and Vanilla:**
   - Beat in the egg and vanilla extract until well combined.
5. **Combine Dry Ingredients:**
   - Gradually add the dry ingredients to the wet mixture, mixing until just combined.
6. **Incorporate Red Bean Paste:**
   - Gently fold the sweet red bean paste into the cookie dough. The red bean paste should be evenly distributed but may create a marbled effect in the dough.
7. **Shape Cookies:**
   - Scoop tablespoon-sized portions of dough and roll them into balls. Place them on the prepared baking sheets, spacing them about 1 inch apart. If desired, you can

gently flatten the balls with the back of a spoon or your fingers. For added texture, you can roll the dough balls in sesame seeds or shredded coconut before baking.

8. **Bake:**
   - Bake in the preheated oven for 10-12 minutes, or until the edges are lightly golden and the centers are set.
9. **Cool:**
   - Allow the cookies to cool on the baking sheets for a few minutes before transferring them to a wire rack to cool completely.
10. **Optional Dusting:**
    - Once cooled, you can dust the cookies with powdered sugar for a touch of sweetness and decoration.

Tips:

- **Red Bean Paste:** You can use store-bought smooth or chunky red bean paste. If using homemade red bean paste, ensure it is well-cooked and not too wet.
- **Texture:** The cookies should have a soft, slightly chewy texture with pockets of sweet red bean paste. If the dough is too soft to handle, chill it in the refrigerator for about 30 minutes.
- **Storage:** Store the cookies in an airtight container at room temperature for up to a week. They can also be frozen for longer storage.

Red Bean Mochi Cookies are a delightful treat that combines the traditional flavors of Japanese mochi with the classic appeal of cookies. Enjoy the unique texture and sweet flavor in every bite!

Shiso and Lime Cookies

Ingredients:

For the Cookies:

- 1 cup (2 sticks, 230g) unsalted butter, softened
- 1 cup (200g) granulated sugar
- 1/2 cup (100g) powdered sugar
- 1 large egg
- 1 teaspoon vanilla extract
- 2 1/4 cups (285g) all-purpose flour
- 1/2 teaspoon baking powder
- 1/4 teaspoon baking soda
- 1/4 teaspoon salt
- **2 tablespoons finely chopped fresh shiso leaves** (or 1 tablespoon dried shiso leaves, crushed)
- **Zest of 1 lime**
- **2 tablespoons fresh lime juice**

For Optional Glaze:

- 1/2 cup powdered sugar
- 1 tablespoon fresh lime juice

Instructions:

1. **Prepare Baking Sheets:**
   - Preheat your oven to 350°F (175°C) and line two baking sheets with parchment paper.
2. **Mix Dry Ingredients:**
   - In a medium bowl, whisk together the flour, baking powder, baking soda, and salt. Set aside.
3. **Cream Butter and Sugars:**
   - In a large bowl, cream together the softened butter, granulated sugar, and powdered sugar until light and fluffy.
4. **Add Egg and Vanilla:**
   - Beat in the egg and vanilla extract until well combined.
5. **Incorporate Lime and Shiso:**
   - Add the lime zest, lime juice, and finely chopped shiso leaves to the butter mixture, mixing until evenly distributed.
6. **Combine Dry Ingredients:**

- Gradually add the dry ingredients to the wet mixture, mixing until just combined. The dough will be soft.
7. **Shape Cookies:**
   - Scoop tablespoon-sized portions of dough and roll them into balls. Place them on the prepared baking sheets, spacing them about 1 inch apart. Flatten each ball slightly with the back of a spoon or your fingers.
8. **Bake:**
   - Bake in the preheated oven for 10-12 minutes, or until the edges are lightly golden and the centers are set.
9. **Cool:**
   - Allow the cookies to cool on the baking sheets for a few minutes before transferring them to a wire rack to cool completely.
10. **Optional Glaze:**
    - For an extra touch of sweetness and flavor, mix the powdered sugar with lime juice to create a glaze. Drizzle or spread the glaze over the cooled cookies.

Tips:

- **Shiso Leaves:** If using fresh shiso leaves, make sure they are finely chopped to evenly distribute their flavor. Dried shiso can also be used but may have a slightly different intensity.
- **Lime Juice:** Fresh lime juice is preferred for the best flavor, but bottled lime juice can be used if necessary.
- **Texture:** The cookies should be tender and slightly crisp around the edges with a soft center. The addition of lime juice makes the dough slightly more delicate, so handle it gently.
- **Storage:** Store the cookies in an airtight container at room temperature for up to a week. They can also be frozen for longer storage.

These Shiso and Lime Cookies are a delightful fusion of Japanese herbs and citrus, offering a fresh and unique flavor experience. Enjoy these with a cup of tea or as a special treat!

Yuzu and White Chocolate Cookies

Ingredients:

For the Cookies:

- **1 cup (2 sticks, 230g) unsalted butter, softened**
- **1 cup (200g) granulated sugar**
- **1/2 cup (100g) packed brown sugar**
- **1 large egg**
- **1 teaspoon vanilla extract**
- **2 1/4 cups (285g) all-purpose flour**
- **1/2 teaspoon baking powder**
- **1/4 teaspoon baking soda**
- **1/4 teaspoon salt**
- **1 tablespoon yuzu zest** (from about 1 yuzu; or use bottled yuzu zest if fresh is not available)
- **2 tablespoons fresh yuzu juice** (or bottled yuzu juice)
- **1 cup (175g) white chocolate chips**

For Optional Topping:

- **Additional white chocolate chips** (for pressing on top)
- **Powdered sugar** (for dusting)

Instructions:

1. **Prepare Baking Sheets:**
    - Preheat your oven to 350°F (175°C) and line two baking sheets with parchment paper.
2. **Mix Dry Ingredients:**
    - In a medium bowl, whisk together the flour, baking powder, baking soda, and salt. Set aside.
3. **Cream Butter and Sugars:**
    - In a large bowl, cream together the softened butter, granulated sugar, and brown sugar until light and fluffy.
4. **Add Egg and Vanilla:**
    - Beat in the egg and vanilla extract until well combined.
5. **Incorporate Yuzu:**
    - Mix in the yuzu zest and yuzu juice until evenly distributed.
6. **Combine Dry Ingredients:**
    - Gradually add the dry ingredients to the wet mixture, mixing until just combined. Fold in the white chocolate chips.

7. **Shape Cookies:**
    - Scoop tablespoon-sized portions of dough and roll them into balls. Place them on the prepared baking sheets, spacing them about 1 inch apart. If desired, press a few additional white chocolate chips on top of each dough ball before baking.
8. **Bake:**
    - Bake in the preheated oven for 10-12 minutes, or until the edges are lightly golden and the centers are set. The cookies will continue to firm up as they cool.
9. **Cool:**
    - Allow the cookies to cool on the baking sheets for a few minutes before transferring them to a wire rack to cool completely.
10. **Optional Dusting:**
    - Once cooled, you can dust the cookies with a little powdered sugar for a touch of sweetness and decoration.

Tips:

- **Yuzu Zest and Juice:** If fresh yuzu is not available, you can use bottled yuzu zest and juice, or substitute with lemon zest and juice for a similar but slightly different flavor.
- **White Chocolate Chips:** Using high-quality white chocolate chips will enhance the overall flavor of the cookies.
- **Texture:** These cookies should be soft and slightly chewy with a rich, creamy texture from the white chocolate. Be careful not to overbake, as the cookies will harden more as they cool.
- **Storage:** Store the cookies in an airtight container at room temperature for up to a week. They can also be frozen for longer storage.

Yuzu and white chocolate cookies offer a delightful combination of citrusy brightness and sweet creaminess, making them a perfect treat for any occasion. Enjoy these unique cookies with a cup of tea or as a special indulgence!

Japanese Green Tea Macarons

Ingredients:

For the Macaron Shells:

- 1 cup (120g) almond flour
- 1 3/4 cups (200g) powdered sugar
- 2 large egg whites (room temperature)
- 1/4 teaspoon cream of tartar
- 1/4 cup (50g) granulated sugar
- 1 tablespoon matcha powder (high-quality for best flavor)

For the Filling:

- 1/2 cup (1 stick, 115g) unsalted butter, softened
- 1 cup (120g) powdered sugar
- 2 tablespoons matcha powder
- 1-2 tablespoons heavy cream (or milk, to reach desired consistency)
- 1 teaspoon vanilla extract

Instructions:

1. **Prepare Baking Sheets:**
   - Preheat your oven to 325°F (165°C) and line two baking sheets with parchment paper. If you have a macaron template, place it under the parchment paper to help with uniform sizing.
2. **Sift Dry Ingredients:**
   - In a medium bowl, sift together the almond flour, powdered sugar, and matcha powder. This ensures that the dry ingredients are well combined and helps to avoid lumps.
3. **Whip Egg Whites:**
   - In a clean, dry bowl, beat the egg whites with a hand mixer or stand mixer on medium speed until foamy. Add the cream of tartar and continue beating until soft peaks form.
   - Gradually add the granulated sugar while continuing to beat, until the meringue forms stiff, glossy peaks.
4. **Fold in Dry Ingredients:**
   - Gently fold the sifted dry ingredients into the meringue using a spatula. Be careful not to overmix. The batter should flow slowly from the spatula and form a ribbon when lifted.
5. **Pipe the Macarons:**

- Transfer the batter to a piping bag fitted with a round tip (about 1/4-inch diameter). Pipe small circles (about 1.5 inches in diameter) onto the prepared baking sheets, spacing them about 1 inch apart. Tap the baking sheets gently on the counter to release any air bubbles.

6. **Rest the Macarons:**
    - Let the piped macarons rest at room temperature for 30-60 minutes, or until the tops are dry to the touch. This helps to form the characteristic macaron "skin."
7. **Bake:**
    - Bake in the preheated oven for 12-15 minutes, or until the macarons have risen and developed a smooth shell. The macarons should not be sticking to the parchment paper when lifted.
8. **Cool:**
    - Allow the macarons to cool completely on the baking sheets before removing them.
9. **Prepare the Filling:**
    - In a medium bowl, beat together the softened butter, powdered sugar, matcha powder, and vanilla extract until smooth. Gradually add heavy cream (or milk) until the filling reaches a creamy, spreadable consistency.
10. **Assemble the Macarons:**
    - Pair up the macaron shells by size. Pipe or spread a small amount of filling onto the flat side of one shell, then sandwich it with another shell. Gently press to spread the filling evenly.
11. **Mature:**
    - For the best flavor and texture, let the assembled macarons mature in the refrigerator for at least 24 hours before serving. This allows the flavors to meld and the filling to soften the shells.

Tips:

- **Macaronage:** The folding process (macaronage) is crucial for achieving the correct texture. The batter should flow slowly but steadily from the spatula. If overmixed, the shells may spread too much and become flat.
- **Matcha Powder:** Use high-quality matcha powder for the best flavor and vibrant color. Lower-quality matcha may taste bitter.
- **Storing:** Store the filled macarons in an airtight container in the refrigerator for up to a week. They can also be frozen for up to a month. Allow them to come to room temperature before serving.

Japanese green tea macarons are a sophisticated and flavorful treat, offering a lovely balance of creamy filling and crisp, delicate shells. Enjoy these elegant cookies with a cup of tea or as a special dessert!

Chestnut and Yuzu Cookies

Ingredients:

For the Cookies:

- **1 cup (2 sticks, 230g) unsalted butter, softened**
- **1 cup (200g) granulated sugar**
- **1/2 cup (100g) packed brown sugar**
- **1 large egg**
- **1 teaspoon vanilla extract**
- **2 1/4 cups (285g) all-purpose flour**
- **1/2 teaspoon baking powder**
- **1/4 teaspoon baking soda**
- **1/4 teaspoon salt**
- **1/2 cup (120g) chestnut puree** (sweetened or unsweetened, depending on preference)
- **2 tablespoons yuzu zest** (from about 1 yuzu; or use bottled yuzu zest if fresh is not available)
- **2 tablespoons fresh yuzu juice** (or bottled yuzu juice)

For Optional Topping:

- **Powdered sugar** (for dusting)
- **Chopped chestnuts** (for garnish, if desired)

Instructions:

1. **Prepare Baking Sheets:**
    - Preheat your oven to 350°F (175°C) and line two baking sheets with parchment paper.
2. **Mix Dry Ingredients:**
    - In a medium bowl, whisk together the flour, baking powder, baking soda, and salt. Set aside.
3. **Cream Butter and Sugars:**
    - In a large bowl, cream together the softened butter, granulated sugar, and brown sugar until light and fluffy.
4. **Add Egg and Vanilla:**
    - Beat in the egg and vanilla extract until well combined.
5. **Incorporate Chestnut and Yuzu:**
    - Mix in the chestnut puree, yuzu zest, and yuzu juice until evenly distributed.
6. **Combine Dry Ingredients:**
    - Gradually add the dry ingredients to the wet mixture, mixing until just combined. The dough should be soft but not too sticky.

7. **Shape Cookies:**
   - Scoop tablespoon-sized portions of dough and roll them into balls. Place them on the prepared baking sheets, spacing them about 1 inch apart. If desired, gently flatten the dough balls with the back of a spoon or your fingers. You can also press a few chopped chestnuts into the top of each cookie for added texture and garnish.
8. **Bake:**
   - Bake in the preheated oven for 10-12 minutes, or until the edges are lightly golden and the centers are set.
9. **Cool:**
   - Allow the cookies to cool on the baking sheets for a few minutes before transferring them to a wire rack to cool completely.
10. **Optional Dusting:**
    - Once cooled, you can dust the cookies with powdered sugar for a touch of sweetness and decoration.

Tips:

- **Chestnut Puree:** Sweetened chestnut puree is commonly used in desserts, but you can use unsweetened if you prefer to control the sweetness. If using unsweetened puree, you might want to adjust the sugar in the recipe slightly.
- **Yuzu:** If fresh yuzu is unavailable, bottled yuzu zest and juice can be used. Alternatively, lemon zest and juice can be substituted for a similar but slightly different citrus flavor.
- **Texture:** These cookies should have a soft, slightly chewy texture with a rich chestnut flavor and a hint of yuzu freshness. Be careful not to overbake to keep them tender.
- **Storage:** Store the cookies in an airtight container at room temperature for up to a week. They can also be frozen for longer storage.

Chestnut and yuzu cookies offer a delightful fusion of nutty and citrus flavors, making them a unique and delicious treat. Enjoy these cookies with a cup of tea or as a special indulgence!

Miso and Caramel Crunch Cookies

Ingredients:

For the Cookies:

- 1 cup (2 sticks, 230g) unsalted butter, softened
- 1 cup (200g) granulated sugar
- 1/2 cup (100g) packed brown sugar
- 1/4 cup (60g) white miso paste (white or yellow miso is preferred for a milder flavor)
- 1 large egg
- 1 teaspoon vanilla extract
- 2 1/4 cups (285g) all-purpose flour
- 1/2 teaspoon baking powder
- 1/4 teaspoon baking soda
- 1/4 teaspoon salt
- 1 cup (100g) caramel bits or chopped caramel candies
- 1/2 cup (50g) crushed pretzels (for crunch, optional)

For Optional Drizzle:

- 1/2 cup (100g) caramel sauce
- 1/4 cup (60g) white chocolate chips (for melting and drizzling, optional)

Instructions:

1. **Prepare Baking Sheets:**
   - Preheat your oven to 350°F (175°C) and line two baking sheets with parchment paper.
2. **Mix Dry Ingredients:**
   - In a medium bowl, whisk together the flour, baking powder, baking soda, and salt. Set aside.
3. **Cream Butter, Sugars, and Miso:**
   - In a large bowl, cream together the softened butter, granulated sugar, brown sugar, and miso paste until light and fluffy.
4. **Add Egg and Vanilla:**
   - Beat in the egg and vanilla extract until well combined.
5. **Combine Dry Ingredients:**
   - Gradually add the dry ingredients to the wet mixture, mixing until just combined. Fold in the caramel bits and crushed pretzels (if using) until evenly distributed.
6. **Shape Cookies:**

- Scoop tablespoon-sized portions of dough and roll them into balls. Place them on the prepared baking sheets, spacing them about 1 inch apart. Flatten each ball slightly with the back of a spoon or your fingers.

7. **Bake:**
    - Bake in the preheated oven for 10-12 minutes, or until the edges are golden and the centers are set. The cookies will continue to firm up as they cool.
8. **Cool:**
    - Allow the cookies to cool on the baking sheets for a few minutes before transferring them to a wire rack to cool completely.
9. **Optional Drizzle:**
    - If desired, melt the white chocolate chips in a microwave-safe bowl in 30-second intervals, stirring until smooth. Drizzle the melted white chocolate over the cooled cookies.
    - Warm the caramel sauce slightly if needed, then drizzle it over the cookies. Let the drizzles set before serving.

Tips:

- **Miso Paste:** White or yellow miso paste is best for a milder, sweeter flavor. Red miso is more robust and might overpower the caramel.
- **Caramel Bits:** You can use store-bought caramel bits or chop up caramel candies. If using soft caramels, be sure they're chopped into small pieces so they distribute well.
- **Crunch:** The crushed pretzels add a nice texture contrast. If you prefer, you can substitute with crushed nuts or just leave them out.
- **Storage:** Store the cookies in an airtight container at room temperature for up to a week. They can also be frozen for longer storage.

Miso and caramel crunch cookies offer a delightful balance of sweet, savory, and crunchy elements, making them a unique and delicious treat. Enjoy them with a cup of tea or as a special dessert!

Sakura and White Chocolate Cookies

Ingredients:

For the Cookies:

- 1 cup (2 sticks, 230g) unsalted butter, softened
- 1 cup (200g) granulated sugar
- 1/2 cup (100g) packed brown sugar
- 1 large egg
- 1 teaspoon vanilla extract
- 2 1/4 cups (285g) all-purpose flour
- 1/2 teaspoon baking powder
- 1/4 teaspoon baking soda
- 1/4 teaspoon salt
- **2 tablespoons sakura (cherry blossom) extract** (or 1-2 tablespoons dried sakura petals, finely chopped)
- 1 cup (175g) white chocolate chips

For Optional Topping:

- **Additional white chocolate chips** (for pressing on top)
- **Powdered sugar** (for dusting)
- **Edible cherry blossoms** (for garnish, if available)

Instructions:

1. **Prepare Baking Sheets:**
   - Preheat your oven to 350°F (175°C) and line two baking sheets with parchment paper.
2. **Mix Dry Ingredients:**
   - In a medium bowl, whisk together the flour, baking powder, baking soda, and salt. Set aside.
3. **Cream Butter and Sugars:**
   - In a large bowl, cream together the softened butter, granulated sugar, and brown sugar until light and fluffy.
4. **Add Egg and Vanilla:**
   - Beat in the egg and vanilla extract until well combined.
5. **Incorporate Sakura Extract:**
   - Mix in the sakura extract (or finely chopped dried sakura petals) until evenly distributed.
6. **Combine Dry Ingredients:**

- Gradually add the dry ingredients to the wet mixture, mixing until just combined. Fold in the white chocolate chips.

7. **Shape Cookies:**
   - Scoop tablespoon-sized portions of dough and roll them into balls. Place them on the prepared baking sheets, spacing them about 1 inch apart. If desired, press a few additional white chocolate chips into the top of each dough ball before baking.
8. **Bake:**
   - Bake in the preheated oven for 10-12 minutes, or until the edges are lightly golden and the centers are set. The cookies will continue to firm up as they cool.
9. **Cool:**
   - Allow the cookies to cool on the baking sheets for a few minutes before transferring them to a wire rack to cool completely.
10. **Optional Garnish:**
    - Once cooled, you can dust the cookies with powdered sugar for a touch of sweetness. If using edible cherry blossoms, gently press them onto the cookies for an elegant finishing touch.

Tips:

- **Sakura Extract:** If sakura extract is unavailable, you can use a small amount of almond or rose extract as a substitute, but this will change the flavor profile. Dried sakura petals can also be used for a more authentic taste and appearance.
- **White Chocolate Chips:** Use high-quality white chocolate chips for the best flavor. If you prefer, you can chop a white chocolate bar instead.
- **Texture:** The cookies should have a soft and slightly chewy texture with bursts of sweet white chocolate. Be careful not to overbake, as they can become too crisp.
- **Storage:** Store the cookies in an airtight container at room temperature for up to a week. They can also be frozen for longer storage.

Sakura and white chocolate cookies are a delicate and delightful treat that captures the essence of spring with every bite. Enjoy these elegant cookies with a cup of tea or as a special treat for any occasion!

Kumquat and Almond Cookies

Ingredients:

For the Cookies:

- 1 cup (2 sticks, 230g) unsalted butter, softened
- 1 cup (200g) granulated sugar
- 1/2 cup (100g) packed brown sugar
- 1 large egg
- 1 teaspoon vanilla extract
- 2 1/4 cups (285g) all-purpose flour
- 1/2 teaspoon baking powder
- 1/4 teaspoon baking soda
- 1/4 teaspoon salt
- 1/2 cup finely chopped kumquats (about 6-8 kumquats, seeds removed)
- 1/2 cup chopped almonds (toasted or raw)

For Optional Glaze:

- 1/2 cup powdered sugar
- **2 tablespoons fresh kumquat juice** (or lemon juice if kumquat is unavailable)
- **1-2 teaspoons milk or water** (to reach desired consistency)

Instructions:

1. **Prepare Baking Sheets:**
   - Preheat your oven to 350°F (175°C) and line two baking sheets with parchment paper.
2. **Prepare Kumquats:**
   - Finely chop the kumquats, removing any seeds. If they are very juicy, you might want to pat them dry with a paper towel to prevent excess moisture in the dough.
3. **Mix Dry Ingredients:**
   - In a medium bowl, whisk together the flour, baking powder, baking soda, and salt. Set aside.
4. **Cream Butter and Sugars:**
   - In a large bowl, cream together the softened butter, granulated sugar, and brown sugar until light and fluffy.
5. **Add Egg and Vanilla:**
   - Beat in the egg and vanilla extract until well combined.
6. **Incorporate Kumquats and Almonds:**
   - Mix in the chopped kumquats and chopped almonds until evenly distributed.
7. **Combine Dry Ingredients:**

- Gradually add the dry ingredients to the wet mixture, mixing until just combined.
8. **Shape Cookies:**
   - Scoop tablespoon-sized portions of dough and roll them into balls. Place them on the prepared baking sheets, spacing them about 1 inch apart. Flatten each ball slightly with the back of a spoon or your fingers.
9. **Bake:**
   - Bake in the preheated oven for 10-12 minutes, or until the edges are lightly golden and the centers are set. The cookies will firm up as they cool.
10. **Cool:**
    - Allow the cookies to cool on the baking sheets for a few minutes before transferring them to a wire rack to cool completely.
11. **Optional Glaze:**
    - In a small bowl, mix the powdered sugar with fresh kumquat juice (or lemon juice) and enough milk or water to achieve a smooth, pourable consistency. Drizzle the glaze over the cooled cookies.

Tips:

- **Kumquats:** If kumquats are not available, you can substitute with finely chopped candied orange peel or another citrus fruit like lemon or lime for a similar tangy flavor.
- **Almonds:** Toasting the almonds before chopping can enhance their flavor, but raw almonds will work as well.
- **Texture:** The cookies should be slightly crunchy around the edges with a tender center. Be cautious not to overbake them to keep them soft and flavorful.
- **Storage:** Store the cookies in an airtight container at room temperature for up to a week. They can also be frozen for longer storage.

Kumquat and almond cookies offer a delightful combination of tangy citrus and nutty richness, making them a refreshing and enjoyable treat. Perfect for a special occasion or as a unique addition to your cookie repertoire!

www.ingramcontent.com/pod-product-compliance
Lightning Source LLC
LaVergne TN
LVHW081558060526
838201LV00054B/1951